Primary Source and Reading Guide

US History

INTERACTIVE

SAVVAS
LEARNING COMPANY

Cover: Declaration of Independence: Popular and applied graphic art print filing series/Library of Congress Prints and Photographs Division Washington, D.C.[LC-DIG-ppmsca-59409]; Massachusetts Spy 1775 revolutionary newspaper: Old Paper Studios/Alamy Stock Photo; United States Constitution: Photo Researchers/Science History Images/Alamy Stock Photo; Post stamp: Ensuper/Shutterstock

Cover Inset: Statue of Liberty: Onehundred Percent/Alamy Stock Photo; Colonial Flag: George Nazlis/Alamy Stock Photo; Hopi Kachina Doll: gary warnimont/Alamy Stock Photo; Young Asian Woman: Muhammad Julian Elit Santosa/Alamy Stock Photo; Young Hispanic Man: cheapbooks/Shutterstock; Liberty Bell: ClassicStock/Alamy Stock Photo; Young African American Man: AJR_photo/Shutterstock; Young Caucasian Woman: mauritius images GmbH/Alamy Stock Photo; Cesar Chavez - Everett Collection Inc/Alamy Stock Photo/TM/© The Cesar Chavez Foundation www.chavezfoundation.org; Conestoga Wagon Wheel: George Sheldon/Shutterstock; Mars Rover Perseverance Simulation: NASA/JPL-Caltech; Harriet Tubman: Science History Images/Alamy Stock Photo

Attributions of third party content appear on pages 320–322, which constitute an extension of this copyright page.

ISBN-13: 978-1-418-33233-4
ISBN-10: 1-418-33233-X

3   21

Topic 1 America's Cultural Roots (Prehistory–1783)

Topic 2 England's American Colonies (1607–1754)

Topic 3 The American Revolution (1754–1783)

Topic 4 Establishing the New Nation (1781–1789)

Topic 5 The Early Republic (1789–1840)

Topic 6 Reshaping America in the Early 1800s (1800–1860)

Topic 7 Sectional Divisions and Civil War (1846–1865)

Topic 8 Reconstruction (1865–1877)

Topic 9 Industry and Immigration (1865–1914)

Topic 10 Changes in the Late 1800 (1865–1900)

Topic 11 America Comes of Age (1890–1920)

Topic 12 World War I and the 1920s (1914–1929)

Topic 13 The Great Depression and the New Deal (1928–1941)

Topic 14 World War II (1931–1945)

Topic 15 Postwar America (1945–1960)

Topic 16 Civil Rights and Reform in the 1960s (1945–1968)

Topic 17 The Vietnam War Era (1954–1975)

CLOSE READING

PRIMARY SOURCE EXPLORATION

Reactions to the Vietnam War

Topic 18 An Era of Change (1960–1980)

CLOSE READING

PRIMARY SOURCE EXPLORATION

Native Americans Fight for Their Rights

Topic 19 America in the 1980s and 1990s (1980–1999)

Topic 20 America in the Twenty-First Century (2000–Today)

Lesson 1 The Peoples of the Americas

CLOSE READING

Early Inhabitants of the Americas

1. **Assess Arguments** There are two major theories about how Paleo-Indians came to North and South America. Some believe they came on foot from Siberia during the Ice Age, while others believe they migrated to the Americas along the coast in boats. Which theory do you find more convincing? Why?

2. **Identify Cause and Effect** Explain how the ice age and the climate change that followed affected the development and settlement of early American Indians.

3. **Identify Supporting Details** Give two examples of how different American Indian groups adapted to the environment around them.

Early Cultures in North America

4. **Identify Supporting Details** Find at least two details or examples that support this main idea: Access to water was essential for American Indians living in the Southwest.

5. Analyze Interactions Give two examples of American Indian societies that experienced a major crisis, and explain the consequences of each crisis.

6. Compare and Contrast Use the graphic organizer below to show the similarities and differences between the American Indians who lived in the Rocky Mountains and those who lived on the Great Plains.

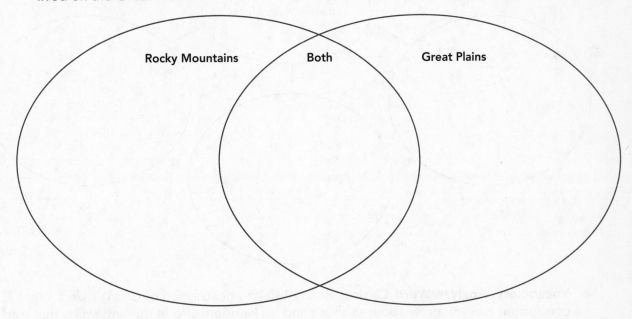

Rocky Mountains   Both   Great Plains

7. Draw Inferences How was the structure of the Iroquois League different from the structure of governments today? How was it similar to other governments?

8. Compare What cultural features did many American Indian groups share?

Lesson 2 The West Africans

CLOSE READING

The Kingdoms of West Africa

1. **Analyze Interactions Among Ideas** As you read this lesson, look for ways West Africa was influenced by Islam. Use the web graphic organizer below to organize facts about Islam in West Africa.

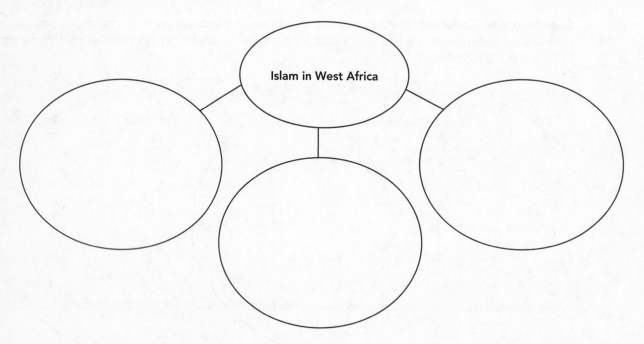

2. **Vocabulary: Analyze Word Choices** Read Al-Bakri's description of Ghana's king. What conclusions can you draw about this king and his kingdom? Point out any words that lead to these conclusions.

3. **Compare and Contrast** Compare and contrast the early kingdoms of West Africa: Ghana, Mali, and Songhai.

Characteristics of West African Societies

4. Compare and Contrast How were West African traditional spiritual beliefs similar to the beliefs of American Indians? How were they different?

5. Summarize Explain how kings in West Africa used land to keep their power.

6. Compare and Contrast How was slavery in West Africa similar to and different from the system of slavery that later became common in North America?

7. Draw Inferences Describe the Portuguese influence on West Africa in the 1400s and 1500s.

Lesson 3 Europeans Make Contact

CLOSE READING

Change Sweeps Through Europe in the 1400s

1. **Compare and Contrast** How was the structure of European society in the 1400s and 1500s similar to the structures of West African societies, which you read about in Lesson 2?

Europe Expands Its Influence

2. **Identify Cause and Effect** Explain some of the lasting effects of the Crusades.

The Portuguese and Spanish Explore New Routes

3. **Determine Central Ideas** What motivated the Portuguese to explore lands to their south and to the east?

4. **Identify Supporting Details** What technological innovations enabled the European explorers to take long voyages?

Christopher Columbus Explores the Americas

5. Compare and Contrast What did Christopher Columbus wish to do with the land he believed he had discovered? What did he actually do? Use the quote from Columbus's journal to support your answer.

The Spanish Build an American Empire

6. Identify Cause and Effect Why did Cortés want to invade the Aztec empire? Why did Moctezuma invite Cortés into Tenochtitlán?

7. Summarize What happened when European diseases reached the Americas? How did this affect the American Indian population?

The Columbian Exchange

8. Cite Evidence Was the Columbian Exchange a positive change? Why or why not?

Lesson 4 Spain and France in the Americas

CLOSE READING

European Rivalries Spread to the Americas

1. **Analyze Interactions Among Ideas and Events** How did the Protestant Reformation affect relationships among the major European nations in the 1500s?

Governing the Spanish American Empire

2. **Compare and Contrast** How were the original people of the Americas treated by the Spanish missionaries? How was this different from their treatment by the *conquistadors*?

3. **Draw Inferences** Why did the Spanish develop the complex *castas* system?

Spanish Explorers Seek Wealth in the North

4. **Cite Evidence** How did the Pueblos view Spanish *conquistadors* and missionaries? Cite evidence to support your ideas.

5. **Determine Central Idea** Why did the Spanish choose to colonize Florida and the Rio Grande Valley?

Colonization and Conflict in New Mexico

6. **Analyze Sequence** Describe the relationship between the Pueblos and the Apaches during and after the revolt against the Spanish.

The French Settle in North America

7. **Analyze Interactions Among Individuals** How did the French treat the local people in Canada? Why?

Living in New France

8. **Summarize** What were the goals of the French in establishing settlements in Canada and Louisiana? Why did the French have trouble expanding these settlements?

PRIMARY SOURCE EXPLORATION

First Encounters: Europeans and Native Americans

Introduction

When European explorers first arrived in North America they brought with them ideas about people who were different: people who looked, lived, or worshiped in unfamiliar ways. These ideas were often unfavorable.

There are only a few directs accounts by Europeans of their first encounters with Native Americans. There are even fewer accounts by Native Americans of their first encounters with Europeans. In this Primary Source Exploration, you'll examine four sources, two by Europeans and two by Native Americans. Each will require extremely careful reading to understand not just what is being said, but also the history of how the source was passed along over time.

Document-Based Writing Activity

Analyze the following four sources and then use information from the documents and your knowledge of world history to write an essay in which you

- Describe how Europeans and Native Americans viewed one another upon their first contacts.
- Hypothesize how these first encounters may have affected the future relationships between the two groups.

Keep in mind that your essay should include an introduction, several paragraphs, and a conclusion. In the body of the essay, use evidence from at least three documents. Support your response with relevant facts, examples, and details. In developing your essay, be sure to keep these general definitions in mind:

- *Describe* means "to illustrate something in words or tell about it."
- *Hypothesize* means "to present facts to try to predict what might happen."

Source 1

Letter to King Francis I of France, Giovanni da Verrazzano, 1524

Verrazzano was an Italian navigator who was hired by France to explore the Atlantic coast of North America. In this letter to the King of France he describes his encounters with Native Americans living in what is today the Canadian province of Nova Scotia.

So we anchored off the coast and sent the small boat in to land. We had seen many people coming to the seashore, but they fled when they saw us approaching; several times they stopped and turned around to look at us in great wonderment. We reassured them with various signs, and some of them came up, showing great delight at seeing us and marveling at our clothes, appearance, and our whiteness; they showed us by various signs where we could most easily secure the boat, and offered us some of their food. We were on land, and I shall now tell Your Majesty briefly what we were able to learn of their life and customs. . . .

When we went farther inland we saw their houses, which are circular in shape, about XIIII to XV paces across, made of bent saplings; they are arranged without any architectural pattern, and are covered with cleverly worked mats of straw which protect them from wind and rain. There is no doubt that if they had the skilled workmen that we have, they would erect great buildings, for the whole maritime coast is full of various blue rocks, crystals, and alabaster, and for such a purpose it has an abundance of ports and shelter for ships. They move these houses from one place to another according to the richness of the site and the season. They need only carry the straw mats, and so they have new houses made in no time at all. In each house there lives a father with a very large family, for in some we saw XXV to XXX people. They live on the same food as the other people—pulse [beans and peas] (which they produce with more systematic cultivation than the other tribes, and when sewing [sowing]they observe the influence of the moon, the rising of the Pleiades, and many other customs derived from the ancients), and otherwise on game and fish. They live a long time, and rarely fall sick; if they are wounded, they cure themselves with fire without medicine; their end comes with old age. We consider them very compassionate and charitable toward their relatives, for they make great lamentations in times of adversity, recalling in their grief all their past happiness. . . .

1. What words does Verrazzano use in the first paragraph to describe the Native Americans' feelings toward the Europeans? How do you think he knows this is how they are feeling?

2. What assumptions is Verrazzano making about the Native Americans' family structure when he describes who lives in each structure? Why do you think he is making such assumptions?

3. What evidence does Verrazzano provide that the American Indians have sophisticated agricultural practices?

Source 2

Painting of the Town of Pomeiock, John White, 1585

John White was an artist and cartographer who accompanied Sir Walter Raleigh on his voyage to the Outer Banks of what is now North Carolina in 1585. His goal was to capture images of the people, plants, and animals of the region in an effort to give those at home in England an accurate picture of a land that was still unknown to them. It is important to note that most of his original drawings were lost but he later reproduced them. This painting shows a Native American village enclosed by a fence of wooden stakes.

1. What is the major focus of this painting?

2. What can you learn about Native Americans from this painting?

3. How would you go about trying to evaluate the accuracy of this painting?

Source 3

First Encounters of the Ho-Chunk Nation and the French, Paul Radin

This excerpt is from an account of the first contact of the Ho-Chunk (Winnebago) with French explorer Jean Nicolet in Green Bay in 1634. It is important to note that this excerpt was related to an ethnologist, or someone who studies cultures, in the early twentieth century.

. . . .Now this is what the old men have said and handed down to us.

Once something appeared in the middle of the lake (Green Bay). They were the French; they were the first to come to the Winnebago. The ship came nearer and the Winnebago went to the edge of the lake with offerings of tobacco and white deerskins. There they stood. When the French were about to come ashore they fired their guns off in the air as a salute to the Indians. The Indians said, "They are thunderbirds." They had never heard the report of a gun before that time and that is why they thought they were thunderbirds.

Then the French landed their boats and came ashore and extended their hands to the Winnebago, and the Indians put tobacco in their hands. The French, of course, wanted to shake hands with the Indians. They did not know what tobacco was, and therefore did not know what to do with it. Some of the Winnebago poured tobacco on their heads, asking them for victory in war. The French tried to speak to them, but they could not, of course, make themselves understood. After a while they discovered that they were without tools, so they taught the Indians how to use an ax and chop a tree down. The Indians, however, were afraid of it, because they thought that the ax was holy. Then the French taught the Indians how to use guns, but they held aloof for a long time through fear, thinking that all these things were holy.

1. How did the Native Amerians perceive the Europeans when they first encountered them, according to this account?

2. How accurate do you think this account is?

3. What questions would you ask the Native American narrator? What questions would you ask the ethnologist who recorded this interview?

Source 4

New Relations of Gaspesia, 1691, Chrestien Le Clercq

This excerpt was written by a French priest who was traveling in what is now eastern Canada. It captures the response of a Micmac Native American leader to the French, who are trying to convince him of the superiority of France and the French way of life.

Since, these people live without society and without commerce, they have neither towns nor villages, unless, indeed, one is willing to call by these names certain collections of wigwams having the forms of tents, very badly kept, and just as badly arranged. . . .

But however that may be, the Indians esteem their camps as much as, and even more than, they do the most superb and commodious [spacious, comfortable] of our houses....having asked me to serve them as interpreter [we] were extremely surprised when the leading Indian, . . .answered me with these words:

. . . Thou art not as bold nor as stout [strong] as we, because when thou goest on a voyage thou canst not carry upon they shoulders thy buildings....As for us, we find ourselves secure from all these inconveniences, and we can always say, more truly than thou, we are at home everywhere, because we set up our wigwams with ease wheresoever we go, and without asking permission of anybody. . . .

As to us, we find all our riches and all our conveniences among ourselves, without trouble and without exposing our lives to the dangers in which you find yourselves constantly through your long voyages. . . .

We see also that all your people live, as a rule, only upon cod which you catch among us. It is everlastingly nothing but cod—cod in the morning, cod at midday, cod at evening, and always cod. . .if you wish some good morsels,. . .you are obliged to have recourse [help from] . . . the Indians, whom you despise so much, and to beg them to go a-hunting that you may be [supplied with food].

1. Why does the leading native man who is speaking to the interpreter believe that their own wigwams are superior to the French houses?

2. Why do you think the Frenchmen were surprised by the native man's comments?

3. Which lines in the excerpt indicate that land in the region is not divided up and privately owned?

Lesson 1 The Southern Colonies Take Root

CLOSE READING

England Establishes Colonies in North America

1. **Draw Inferences** Why do you think that English businessmen and joint-stock companies believed they had the right to send settlers to colonize Native American land?

2. **Draw Conclusions** Why did the Powhatan allow English settlers to gain a foothold in the Chesapeake Bay area?

Early Challenges in Jamestown

3. **Summarize** How did the English government profit from the success of Jamestown?

4. **Draw Inferences** In what way did the establishment of the House of Burgesses signify a weakening of the power of the Virginia Company over the colonists?

Expansion in Virginia Creates Conflict

5. Identify Main Ideas Use this flowchart to show the sequence of events in Bacon's Rebellion.

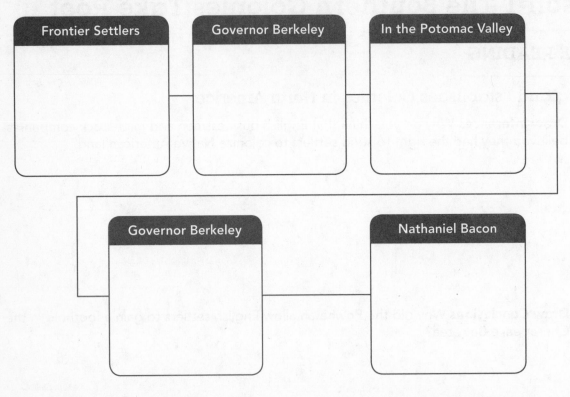

Frontier Settlers	Governor Berkeley	In the Potomac Valley

Governor Berkeley	Nathaniel Bacon

6. Summarize What did Bacon's Rebellion reveal about social tensions developing in Virginia?

England Expands Its Southern Colonies

7. Identify Cause and Effect Why did slavery emerge as a political issue in the early colony of Georgia?

Lesson 2 New Lives in New England

CLOSE READING

Disagreement with the Church of England

1. Identify Main Ideas Why did the king and the Church of England view the Puritans as a threat?

2. Draw Inferences What did the Puritans hope to establish in America?

3. Summarize Summarize the main reason the Puritans left England for America.

Puritans Arrive in North America

4. Identify Cause and Effect How did religious disagreement among the Puritans of Massachusetts help launch other colonies in New England?

5. **Summarize** Why did Rhode Islanders separate church and state?

6. **Draw Inferences** What does the Puritan persecution of dissenters and the witch hysteria reveal about Puritan society?

English Relationships with American Indians

7. **Compare and Contrast** How did the differing English and Native American views of the natural world lead to cultural conflict?

8. **Make Inferences** What surprised Native Americans about the English settlers' methods of warfare?

Lesson 3 The Middle Colonies Thrive

CLOSE READING

New Netherland and Its Neighbors

1. **Cite Evidence** Why did the Dutch found New Amsterdam?

2. **Draw Inferences** Why do you think the colony of New Netherland was so tolerant of religious diversity?

3. **Evaluate Explanations** What economic tensions led to war between England and the Netherlands?

4. **Draw Inferences** Why do you think settlers in New Jersey were allowed religious freedom?

Religious Toleration in Pennsylvania

5. Draw Inferences What Quaker beliefs and practices would have most troubled Puritans?

6. Compare and Contrast Fill in the table to show how the Middle Colonies differed from New England.

	Middle Colonies	New England
Religion		
Ethnicity		

7. Draw Conclusions How did settlers in Pennsylvania avoid conflict with Native Americans?

Lesson 4 Immigration and Slavery in the Colonies

CLOSE READING

Immigrants Populate the Colonies

1. **Cite Evidence** On the timeline, show how changes in the English economy affected English immigration to the colonies in the 1600s.

2. **Identify Cause and Effect** What political event allowed the Scots to gain easier access to the colonies after 1707?

3. **Summarize** What "pull factors" drew Germans to Pennsylvania?

Enslaved Africans Provide Labor

4. **Identify Cause and Effect** What was the relationship between the expansion of slavery and changes in English patterns of immigration?

5. **Draw Inferences** What does the dependence on indentured servants and enslaved people reveal about the size and nature of the colonial labor force?

6. **Draw Conclusions** What effect did the growing number of enslaved people have on the wealth of the colonies?

Africans in the American Colonies

7. **Evaluate Explanations** Why did the Spanish in Florida offer freedom to enslaved people from the British colonies?

8. **Cite Evidence** How did a minority of enslaved African Americans gain freedom?

Lesson 5 Economic and Social Life in the Colonies

CLOSE READING

England and Its Colonial Economy

1. **Compare and Contrast** Use the chart to compare the relationship between available farmland and population in England and its colonies.

	England	The colonies
Farmland		
Population		

2. **Identify Cause and Effect** How did the English use the colonies to develop a strong navy?

3. **Determine Central Ideas** How did transatlantic trade increase the size of the enslaved population in the colonies?

Regional Economic Differences

4. **Compare and Contrast** How did climate affect the economies of New England and the Middle Colonies?

5. **Determine Central Ideas** Why did an economy based on cash crops and slavery develop in the southern colonies?

Regional Social Differences

6. **Evaluate Explanations** Why did the Middle Colonies become the most ethnically and culturally diverse region in the British empire?

7. **Compare and Contrast** Why did greater economic inequalities develop in the South compared to New England?

8. **Identify Cause and Effect** How did the religious practices in New England help create a more literate and educated population?

Lesson 6 Creating an American Identity

CLOSE READING

Early Government in the Colonies

1. **Compare and Contrast** Why did the English monarch have so little direct control over colonial affairs (in contrast to the control that the French and Spanish monarchs had over their colonies)?

2. **Determine Central Ideas** What political principles did the colonists bring with them from England?

3. **Draw Conclusions** Fill in this concept web to show how the English Bill of Rights strengthened and extended the rights established in the Magna Carta.

English Bill of Rights

New Ideas Empower Individuals

4. **Draw Inferences** In what ways did advances in science influence political thought during the Enlightenment?

5. **Determine Central Ideas** How did John Locke challenge both the authority of kings and of the church?

The Great Awakening

6. **Draw Inferences** What does the Great Awakening reveal about colonists' attitudes to the services of the established churches?

7. **Cite Evidence** Why were the religious revivals of the Great Awakening held in locations such as open fields, rather than inside churches?

8. **Draw Conclusions** How did the Great Awakening challenge existing social and religious structures in the colonies?

PRIMARY SOURCE EXPLORATION

Religious Toleration in the English Colonies

Introduction

Seventeenth-century Europe was torn by religious strife. Protestants fought Catholics while Protestants themselves splintered into opposing denominations or sects. Meanwhile, governments took sides, championing one faith or another. This practice of a government or state supporting an "established" church and persecuting dissenters was transplanted to the American colonies. In time, religious freedom prevailed, but the path to toleration was not easy.

Document-Based Writing Activity

Analyze the following four sources and then use information from the documents and your knowledge of American history to write an essay in which you

- Describe the religious establishments that were set up in various colonies.
- Discuss why the issue of religious toleration was so important to the colonists.

Keep in mind that your essay should include an introduction, several paragraphs, and a conclusion. In the body of the essay, be sure to present evidence from the viewpoints on both sides of the issue, using at least three documents. Support your response with relevant facts, examples, and details. In developing your essay, be sure to keep these general definitions in mind:

- *Describe* means "to illustrate something in words or tell about it."
- *Discuss* means "to make observations about something using facts, reasoning, and argument; to present in some detail."

Source 1

The Bloudy Tenent of Persecution for Cause of Conscience, *Roger Williams, 1644*

Early arguments for toleration came from Roger Williams, a minister who was forced out of the Massachusetts Bay Colony by Puritan authorities. Williams founded the colony of Rhode Island and waged a war of words with the Puritans. In 1644 he published *The Bloudy* [bloody] *Tenent* [tenet] *of Persecution for Cause of Conscience*. In the book, Williams demands that governments stop persecuting religious minorities, including Catholics, Jews, Muslims, and pagans and calls for a "wall of separation" to divide church from state. This excerpt from the preface summarizes the arguments of the book.

Preface:

First. That the blood of so many hundred thousand souls of protestants and papists [Catholics], spilt in the wars of present and former ages, for their respective consciences, is not required nor accepted by Jesus Christ the Prince of Peace.

Secondly. Pregnant scriptures and arguments are throughout the work proposed against the doctrine of persecution for cause of conscience.

Thirdly. Satisfactory answers are given to scriptures and objections produced by Mr. Calvin, Beza, Mr. Cotton, and the ministers of the New English churches, and others former and later, tending to prove the doctrine of persecution for cause of conscience.

Fourthly. The doctrine of persecution for cause of conscience, is proved guilty of all the blood of the souls crying for vengeance under the altar.

Fifthly. All civil states, with their officers of justice, in their respective constitutions and administrations, are proved essentially civil, and therefore not judges, governors, or defenders of the spiritual, or Christian, state and worship….

Eighthly. God requireth not an uniformity of religion to be enacted and enforced in any civil state; which enforced uniformity, sooner or later, is the greatest occasion of civil war, ravishing of conscience, persecution of Christ Jesus in his servants, and of the hypocrisy and destruction of millions of souls.

1. In the first point, what is Williams saying about the religious wars that were causing so many casualties?

2. In the fifth point, what is Williams saying about civil governments and spiritual leaders?

3. In the eighth point, what according to Williams, are the consequences of "uniformity of religion" or the practice of forcing all people to follow the same religion?

Source 2

The Simple Cobler of Aggawam in America, *Nathaniel Ward, 1647*

The Puritans came to America in search of religious freedom for themselves, but not for others. Taxpayers were expected to support the colony's established church, which often persecuted other religious sects. The Puritans quickly gained a reputation for intolerance, particularly of the Quakers, many of whom they imprisoned or executed. Here the Puritan minister Nathaniel Ward responds to accusations of Puritan intolerance.

[Original spellings have been retained.]

First, such as have given or taken any unfriendly reports of us New-English, should doe well to recollect themselves. Wee have beene reputed a Colluvies [collection] of wild Opinionists, swarmed into a remote wilderness to find elbow-roome for our phanatick [fanatic] Doctrines and practices. . . . I dare take upon me, to bee the Herald of New-England so farre, as to proclaime to the world, in the name of our Colony, that all Familists, Antinomians, Anabaptists, and other Enthusiasts [Puritan names for other Protestant groups] shall have free Liberty to keepe away from us, and such as will come to be gone as fast as they can, the sooner the better. . . .

Concerning tolerations I may further assert. . .

He that is willing to tolerate any Religion, or discrepant way of Religion, beside his own, unless it be in matters meerly indifferent, either doubts of his own, or is not sincere in it.

He that is willing to tolerate any unsound Opinion, that his own may also be tolerated, though never so sound, will for a need hang Gods Bible at the Devills girdle. . . .

It is said, That Men ought to have Liberty of their Conscience, and that it is persecution to debarre them of it: I can rather stand amazed then reply to this: it is an astonishment to think that the braines of men should be parboiled in such impious ignorance; Let all the wits under the Heavens lay their heads together and find an Assertion worse then this (one excepted) I will petition to be chosen the universall Idiot of the world. . .

---

1. Ward begins by mocking critics of the "New English" Puritans. What do these critics' "unfriendly reports" say about the Puritans of New England?

2. What "free Liberty" does Ward offer to other religious groups?

3. What does Ward think about people who tolerate religious opinions that differ from his own?

Source 3

"A Letter Concerning Toleration" John Locke, 1689

The issue of toleration preoccupied people in the British Isles and the colonies throughout the 1600s—a time of civil and religious conflict and unrest. John Locke, the influential philosopher and writer, presented powerful arguments in support of tolerance and against religious persecution.

Honoured Sir, Since you are pleased to inquire what are my thoughts about the mutual toleration of Christians in their different professions of religion, I must needs answer you freely that I esteem toleration to be the chief characteristic mark of the true Church.

For whatsoever some people boast of the antiquity of places and names, or of the pomp of their outward worship; others, of the reformation of their discipline; all, of the orthodoxy [conforming to established principles] of their faith—for everyone is orthodox to himself— these things, and all others of this nature, are much rather marks of men striving for power and empire over one another than of the Church of Christ. Let anyone have never so true a claim to all these things, yet if he be destitute of [lacking in] charity, meekness, and good- will in general towards all mankind, even to those that are not Christians, he is certainly yet short of being a true Christian himself. . .

If the Gospel and the apostles may be credited, no man can be a Christian without charity and without that faith which works, not by force, but by love. Now, I appeal to the consciences of those that persecute, torment, destroy and kill other men on the pretence of religion, whether they do it out of friendship and kindness towards them or no?. . .

I esteem it above all things necessary to distinguish exactly the business of civil government from that of religion and to settle the just bounds that lie between the one and the other. If this is not done, there can be no end put to the controversies that will be always arising between those that have, or at least pretend to have, on the one side, a concernment for the interest of men's souls, and, on the other side, a care of the commonwealth.

1. What does Locke mean by "for everyone is orthodox to himself"?

2. What springs to Locke's mind when he hears people boasting about the superiority of their faith over all other faiths?

3. According to the final paragraph in this excerpt, what is the proper relationship between church and state?

Source 4

Church Establishment Table

In each colonial region, settlers approached the decision to set up an established church differently. In New England, the Puritans came to describe their church as "Congregational," because it was made up of self-governing congregations. In contrast, the Anglican church (or Church of England), was governed by a hierarchy of bishops. Gradually, support for tolerance grew, first in Rhode Island and then throughout the Middle Colonies. The colonial world was changing, as a more diverse society emerged.

Church Establishment	Description	Colonies
Congregational	Self-governing congregations	Massachusetts, New Hampshire, Connecticut
Anglican	Ruled by hierarchy of bishops	Virginia, Maryland, North Carolina, South Carolina, Georgia, New York
No established church mandated	Tolerated religious choice	Rhode Island, Pennsylvania, Delaware, New Jersey

1. Study the chart above and remember what you have learned about the three colonial regions. Which established church dominated the southern colonies?

2. Which religious establishment dominated the New England colonies?

3. Which region had colonies in which settlers enjoyed the greatest amount of religious freedom and no established church?

4. Although New York became dominated by the Anglican church after the British takeover from the Dutch, other Protestant sects were tolerated. Based on your knowledge of colonial history, why do you think this happened?

Lesson 1 The French and Indian War

CLOSE READING

Competition for North American Colonies

1. **Draw Inferences** Why did so many Native Americans ally with the French in the French and Indian War? Give a few reasons.

2. **Determine Author's Point of View** Reread the quote from the Iroquois leader, Canasatego. What beliefs about the land did he express?

An Important British Victory

3. **Determine Central Ideas** What was the most significant point of conflict between the British and the French in the 1600s and 1700s? Why?

4. **Identify Cause and Effect** What key move led to the British gaining an advantage and eventually winning the French and Indian War in North America?

5. **Draw Inferences** The war between the French and British wasn't just fought in North America. How do you think this fact affected how the French and the British fought the war?

Pontiac's Rebellion

6. **Draw Inferences** What factors brought an end to Pontiac's Rebellion?

7. **Draw Conclusions** Despite the efforts of the British government, many colonists ignored the Proclamation of 1763. What did this show about the relationship between the British government and the American colonists?

8. **Analyze Cause and Effect** Why did the British impose new taxes on the American colonists during the 1760s?

Lesson 2 Causes of the Revolution

CLOSE READING

The Foundations of Colonial Government

1. **Compare and Contrast** Use the graphic organizer below to show the differences between the British government and American colonial governments in the 1700s. Include information about who led the government, how legislators were chosen, and who was able to vote.

British Government	American Colonies

2. **Explain an Argument** Why did the British believe they had the right to levy taxes on the American colonists? Why did the colonists believe these taxes were unjust?

New Taxes Create Conflict

3. **Draw Conclusions** How do you think the British government could have acted differently so as not to create so much resentment among the colonists? Explain.

Opposition to Taxes Strengthens

4. Analyze Interactions Among Individuals, Events, and Ideas How did Enlightenment ideals influence the American colonists?

5. Compare and Contrast How did the Sons of Liberty and the Daughters of Liberty protest British rule in different ways?

Protests Lead to Violence

6. Identify Cause and Effect Why did the colonists dump tea into the Boston Harbor during the Boston Tea Party?

The First Continental Congress

7. Draw Conclusions What were the Coercive Acts, and why did the colonists consider them "intolerable"?

Lesson 3 The Colonists Declare Independence

CLOSE READING

The First Shots Are Fired

1. **Identify Cause and Effect** In what way were the battles of Lexington and Concord a success for the Patriots?

2. **Draw Conclusions** The opening shot at Lexington and Concord is sometimes called "the shot heard 'round the world." What do you think this means?

Colonists Disagree Over British Rule

3. **Paraphrase** Analyze the Loyalist quote in the first paragraph under this heading. Then summarize in your own words how the Loyalists felt about the Patriots and why they felt this way.

4. **Compare and Contrast** How did the Patriots stereotype the Loyalists? Who were the Loyalists in reality?

5. **Summarize** Why did many Native Americans and enslaved people oppose the Patriots?

6. **Identify Supporting Details** Which Patriot actions may have discouraged some Loyalists from changing their beliefs?

The Decision to Declare Independence

7. **Explain an Argument** According to Thomas Paine, "The cause of America is in a great measure the cause of all mankind." Explain what he meant by this. Was he right? Explain why or why not.

8. **Cite Evidence** In the Declaration of Independence, Thomas Jefferson stated that "all men are created equal." Did the colonies live up to this ideal at the time?

Lesson 4 Americans Win the Revolution

CLOSE READING

The War Begins

1. **Categorize** Use the graphic organizer below to make bulleted lists of mistakes and the victories of the British army during the Revolutionary War. Fill in the graphic organizer as you read all the texts in this lesson.

British Mistakes	British Victories
•	•
•	•
•	•
•	•

The War in the Middle States and Frontier

2. **Draw Inferences** How did France benefit from allying with the American colonists? How did the Americans benefit?

3. **Analyze Interactions Among Individuals and Events** Explain the role of the American Indians in the Revolutionary War.

The War in the South

4. Identify Supporting Details What obstacles did the British army face in the South?

5. Draw Conclusions Explain how the following quote changes or adds to your understanding of the Revolutionary War: "This country is the scene of the most cruel events. Neighbors are on opposite sides, children are against their fathers."

The War Comes to a Conclusion

6. Cite Evidence Explain why Benjamin Franklin was a key figure in the American Revolution. What were some of his contributions?

The Impact of the Revolution

7. Draw Conclusions Why did the American Revolution have a different impact on African Americans in the North and in the South?

PRIMARY SOURCE EXPLORATION

Winning the Revolutionary War

Introduction

In 1775, when George Washington took command of the newly formed Continental Army, he faced a daunting situation. Not only was he fighting Europe's most powerful empire, but he barely had a functioning army. The collection of undisciplined militiamen under his command needed to be organized, trained, and supplied before it could defeat the British. And it needed the help of France and Spain, whose aid made victory possible.

Document-Based Writing Activity

Analyze the following four sources and then use information from the documents and your knowledge of American history to write an essay in which you

- Discuss the experiences of ordinary soldiers during the Revolutionary War.
- Describe how the United States won its independence.

Keep in mind that your essay should include an introduction, several paragraphs, and a conclusion. In the body of the essay, use evidence from at least three documents. Support your response with relevant facts, examples, and details. In developing your essay, be sure to keep these general definitions in mind:

- *Discuss* means "to make observations about something using facts, reasoning, and argument; to present in some detail."
- *Describe* means "to illustrate something in words or tell about it."

Source 1

Wanted for the Continental Army, 1775

Throughout the war, supply was a problem for the Continental Army. The new nation struggled to pay, feed, and arm its troops. Generals, including George Washington, complained bitterly about the lack of supplies. Soldiers wrote of regularly going hungry. Meanwhile, their British enemies had been fighting wars on different continents for a century and were much better equipped.

The Continental Army was formed in June, 1775. In August of that year, the following request for supplies for the new army was printed. Among the goods requested were firewood, corn, oats, shovels, and axes.

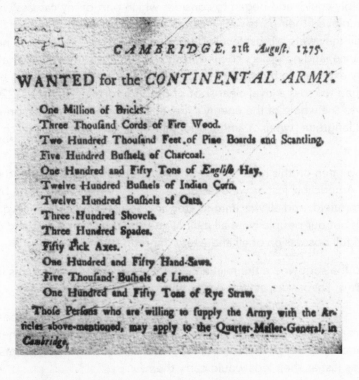

CAMBRIDGE, 21ft Auguft, 1775.

WANTED for the CONTINENTAL ARMY.

One Million of Bricks.
Three Thousand Cords of Fire Wood.
Two Hundred Thousand Feet of Pine Boards and Scantling,
Five Hundred Bushels of Charcoal.
One Hundred and Fifty Tons of English Hay,
Twelve Hundred Bushels of Indian Corn,
Twelve Hundred Bushels of Oats,
Three Hundred Shovels.
Three Hundred Spades.
Fifty Pick Axes.
One Hundred and Fifty Hand-Saws.
Five Thousand Bushels of Lime.
One Hundred and Fifty Tons of Rye Straw.

Those Persons who are willing to supply the Army with the Articles above-mentioned, may apply to the Quarter-Master-General, in Cambridge.

1. What needs would have been filled by these supplies?

2. What else might the army need beyond what is on this list? Why do you think those items were not included?

3. How do you predict difficulty supplying the troops will affect the Continental Army?

Source 2

A Narrative of Some of the Adventures, Dangers and Sufferings of a Revolutionary Soldier, Interspersed with Anecdotes of Incidents that Occurred Within His Own Observation, Joseph Plumb Martin, 1830

Decades after the war, veteran Continental soldier Joseph Plumb Martin recorded his memories of the war. The selection below describes his experiences during the loss of New York City and surrounding areas to the British in 1776.

[A]ll of a sudden, there came such a peal of thunder from the British shipping that I thought my head would go with the sound. I made a frog's leap for the ditch, and lay as still as I possibly could, and began to consider which part of my carcass was to go first. The British played their parts well; indeed, they had nothing to hinder them. We kept the lines till they were almost levelled upon us, when our officers, seeing we could make no resistance, and no orders coming from any superior officer, and that we must soon be entirely exposed to the rake of their guns, gave the order to leave the lines. In retreating, we had to cross a level clear spot of ground, forty or fifty rods [220-275 yards] wide, exposed to the whole of the enemy's fire; and they gave it to us in prime order; the grape shot and langrage [types of ammunition] flew merrily, which served to quicken our motions. . . .

We had not long been on this road before we saw another party, just ahead of us, whom we knew to be Americans; just as we overtook these, they were fired upon by a party of British from a cornfield, and all was immediately in confusion again. I believe the enemies' party was small; but our people were all militia, and the demons of fear and disorder seemed to take full possession of all and every thing on that day.

When I came to the spot where the militia were fired upon, the ground was literally covered with arms, knapsacks, staves, coats, hats. . .

We soon came in sight of a large party of Americans, ahead of us, who appeared to have come into this road by some other rout[e]; we were within sight of them when they were fired upon by another party of the enemy; they returned but a very few shots and then scampered off as fast as their legs would carry them. . . .

---

1. Why was the ground covered with arms and other supplies in the spot Martin saw?

2. Describe the state of the Continental Army during this battle in one word, and explain why you picked it.

3. How does the British army perform during this battle, according to Martin?

Source 3

Regulations for the Order and Discipline of the Troops of the United States, Friedrich Wilhelm Von Steuben, 1779

Joseph Plumb Martin, the author of Source 2, wrote of being constantly made to train in 1778, following the exercises of Baron Von Steuben. The baron was a veteran officer in the Prussian military who was appointed to oversee the training of Continental troops according to the latest European methods. He published his guide for military training in 1779. Known as the Blue Book, it was used by the U.S. military through 1814.

INSTRUCTION FOR THE PRIVATE SOLDIER

The recruit having received his necessaries, should in the first place learn to dress himself with a soldier-like air. To place his effects properly in his knapsack, so as to carry them with ease and convenience; how to salute his officers when he meets them; to clean his arms, wash his linen and cook his provisions. He should early accustom himself to dress in the night; and for that purpose always have his effects in his knapsack, and that placed where he can put his hand on it in a moment, that in case of alarm he may repair with the greatest alertness to the parade.

When learning to march, he must take the greatest pains to acquire a firm step and proper balance, practicing himself at all his leisure hours. He must accustom himself to the greatest steadiness under arms, to pay attention to the commands of his officers, and exercise himself continually with his firelock [gun], in order to acquire vivacity [liveliness] in his motions. He must acquaint himself with the usual beats and signals of the drum, and instantly obey them.

When in the ranks, he must always learn the names of his right and left hand men and file-leader, that he may be able to find his place readily in case of separation. He must cover his file-leader and dress well in his rank, which he may be assured of doing when he can just perceive the breast of the third man from him. Having joined his company, he must no longer consider himself as a recruit, but as a soldier; and whenever he is ordered under arms, must appear well dressed, with his arms, and accoutrements clean and in good order, and his knapsack, blanket &c. ready to throw on his back in case he should be ordered to take them. . . .

1. What is the first thing a private must learn? Why do you think this is so?

2. What are some of the tasks of private soldiers? What does this suggest about soldiers' lives?

3. What was the goal of Von Steuben's regulations? How did he aim to help the war effort?

Source 4

A Narrative of Some of the Adventures, Dangers and Sufferings of a Revolutionary Soldier, Interspersed with Anecdotes of Incidents that Occurred Within His Own Observation, Joseph Plumb Martin, 1830

Martin continued to serve in the Continental Army through the end of the war. In this selection, he recounts his experience at the Battle of Yorktown in 1781.

Here again we encountered our old associate, hunger; affairs, as they respected provisions, &c. were not yet regulated,—no eatable stores had arrived, nor could we expect they should until we knew what reception the enemy would give us. We were, therefore, compelled to try our hands at foraging again. We, that is, our corps of Miners, were encamped near a large wood; there was a plenty of [young pigs] all about this wood, fat and plump, weighing, generally, from fifty to a hundred pounds apiece. We soon found some of them, and as no owner appeared to be at hand, and the hogs not understanding our enquiries (if we made any) sufficiently to inform us to whom they belonged, we made free with some of them to satisfy the calls of nature till we could be better supplied, if better we could be. Our officers countenanced [allowed] us, and that was all the permission we wanted; and many of us did not want even that. . . .

I do not remember, exactly, the number of days we were employed before we got our batteries [artillery] in readiness to open upon the enemy, but think it was not more than two or three. The French, who were upon our left, had completed their batteries a few hours before us, but were not allowed to discharge their pieces till the American batteries were ready. Our commanding battery was on the near bank of the river and contained ten heavy guns; the next was a bomb-battery of three large mortars [a type of cannon]; and so on through the whole line; the whole number, American and French, was, ninety-two cannon, mortars and howitzers [another type of cannon]. Our flagstaff [flagpole] was in the ten gun battery, upon the right of the whole. I was in the trenches the day that the batteries were to be opened; all were upon the tiptoe of expectation and impatience to see the signal given to open the whole line of batteries, which was to be the hoisting of the American flag in the ten gun battery. About noon the much wished for signal went up. I confess I felt a secret pride swell my heart when I saw the "star spangled banner" waving majestically in the very faces of our implacable adversaries; it appeared like an omen of success to our enterprize, and so it proved in reality. A simultaneous discharge of all the guns in the line followed; the French troops accompanying it with "Huzza for the Americans!"

---

1. Does Martin have all the supplies he needs? What has the Continental Army failed to do?

2. Does the Continental Army seem prepared to capture the British fort they are attacking in the second paragraph? Why or why not?

3. How has the situation for the Continental Army changed since Martin fought in New York?

Lesson 1 The Articles of Confederation

CLOSE READING

The States Create Republics

1. **Compare and Contrast** Explain the difference between a unicameral and a bicameral legislature, including the advantages of each.

2. **Cite Evidence** Why did some political leaders oppose allowing all men to vote? Cite evidence to support your answer.

Union Under the Articles of Confederation

3. **Cite Evidence** In what ways did the Articles of Confederation limit the power of the federal government?

The Northwest Territory

4. **Identify Supporting Details** The Northwest Ordinance of 1787 was an important piece of legislature that had a significant impact on the development of the United States. Give three details that support this main idea.

Relations With Foreign Powers

5. Draw Conclusions Explain how the British treated the American colonies after the Revolutionary War.

6. Draw Inferences Why was New Orleans an important city for Americans in the late 1700s?

Weaknesses of the Articles of Confederation

7. Identify Cause and Effect What chain of events led to America's near bankruptcy in the years after the Revolutionary War?

8. Paraphrase What did James Madison mean when he said, "Liberty may be endangered by the abuses of liberty as well as [by] the abuses of power." Cite at least one example that supports Madison's position.

Lesson 2 The Constitutional Convention

CLOSE READING

Leaders Assemble at the Convention

1. **Compare and Contrast** Use the graphic organizer below to take notes about the views of Alexander Hamilton and James Madison.

Alexander Hamilton	James Madison

2. **Determine Central Ideas** What weaknesses of the Articles of Confederation did the Constitutional Convention hope to address?

3. **Draw Conclusions** Consider the men who gathered for the Constitutional Convention. What were the possible strengths and weaknesses of this group?

Constitutional Compromises

4. **Compare and Contrast** Use the chart below to show the key parts of the Virginia and the New Jersey plans. Include information about who presented each plan and how the presidency, the legislature, and the power of the federal and state governments would work under the plan. Then, write an * beside any part of either plan that has lasted until today.

Virginia Plan	New Jersey Plan

5. **Vocabulary: Determine Meaning** What is a *stalemate*? Why did the delegates want to prevent a stalemate in the Constitutional Convention?

6. **Analyze Interactions Among Individuals, Events, and Ideas** How did the Three-Fifths Compromise affect the institution of slavery in subsequent years?

Lesson 3 The Enduring Constitution

CLOSE READING

The Debate Over Ratification

1. **Analyze Style and Rhetoric** Reread the quote by James Lincoln from South Carolina. What was his main idea? What language did he use to support this idea?

2. **Compare and Contrast** Use the graphic organizer below to take notes on the important arguments made by the Federalists and Antifederalists. Include information about how both sides convinced state ratifying committees to support or oppose the Constitution.

Federalists	Antifederalists

3. **Draw Inferences** Why did many farmers oppose the Constitution? What inferences can you make about American farmers in the 1780s?

Ratifying Conventions in the States

4. **Cite Evidence** What actions did the Federalists take to convince the states to ratify the Constitution?

Constitutional Principles

5. **Vocabulary: Determine Meaning** In what way was the Constitution an example of *popular sovereignty*?

6. **Synthesize** How did the ratified Constitution reflect the views of both Federalists and Antifederalists?

7. **Explain** In what ways did the Constitution "insulate" the government from the people?

PRIMARY SOURCE EXPLORATION

The Debate Over the Importation of Enslaved People

Introduction

As the summer of 1787 wore on, delegates to the Constitutional Convention debated one issue after another. Each stood in turn to make his argument and stood again to refute or support a statement made by another delegate. The process was slow, but fascinating. Little by little, the Constitution gradually began to take shape. By late August, it was time to face perhaps the thorniest problem yet: How would it affect the ability of the states to import enslaved people if Congress was to be given the power to regulate international trade?

The southern workforce included more than 500,000 enslaved people and many of the delegates themselves were enslavers. In Georgia, a full 35 percent of the population was enslaved. Many delegates, however, were deeply troubled by the institution of slavery. The debate stretched over several days, with delegates from the northern and southern states locked in a verbal sparring match. In the end, it was decided that the Constitution would allow Congress to ban the importation of enslaved people—but not until the year 1808.

Document-Based Writing Activity

Analyze the following four sources and then use information from the documents and your knowledge of American history to write an essay in which you

- Describe the main arguments made by each side in the debate.
- Discuss why the delegates were motivated to compromise on this issue.

Keep in mind that your essay should include an introduction, several paragraphs, and a conclusion. In the body of the essay, use evidence from at least three documents. Support your response with relevant facts, examples, and details. In developing your essay, be sure to keep these general definitions in mind:

- *Describe* means "to illustrate something in words or tell about it."
- *Discuss* means "to make observations about something using facts, reasoning, and argument; to present in some detail."

Source 1

Notes on the Debates in the Federal Convention, James Madison, 1787

Article 7, Section 4 of the new Constitution stipulated that Congress could not tax or prohibit "the migration or importation of such persons as the several States shall think proper to admit." Everyone at the convention understood that "such persons" referred to enslaved people and that this limitation of congressional powers allowed the importation of enslaved people to continue unhindered for all time. Below is a portion of the debate on this issue.

WEDNESDAY, August 23. In Convention. — Article 7, sect. 4, was resumed.

Mr. SHERMAN [CT] was for leaving the clause as it stands. He disapproved of the slave trade; yet as the States were now possessed of the right to import slaves, as the public good did not require it to be taken from them, & as it was expedient to have as few objections as possible to the proposed scheme of Government, he thought it best to leave the matter as we find it. . . .

Col. MASON [VA] . . . Every master of slaves is born a petty tyrant. They bring the judgment of heaven on a Country. . . . He held it essential in every point of view that the Genl. Govt. should have power to prevent the increase of slavery.

Gen. PINCKNEY [SC] declared it to be his firm opinion that if himself & all his colleagues were to sign the Constitution & use their personal influence, it would be of no avail towards obtaining the assent of their Constituents. S. Carolina & Georgia cannot do without slaves. . . . He contended that the importation of slaves would be for the interest of the whole Union. The more slaves, the more produce to employ the carrying [export] trade; The more consumption also, and the more of this, the more of revenue for the common treasury. . . .

Mr. RUTLEDGE [SC] If the Convention thinks that N. C., S. C., & Georgia will ever agree to the plan, unless their right to import slaves be untouched, the expectation is vain. The people of those States will never be such fools as to give up so important an interest. . . .

Mr. RANDOLPH [VA] was for committing [sending the clause to a subcommittee] in order that some middle ground might, if possible, be found. He could never agree to the clause as it stands. He would sooner risk the constitution. He dwelt on the dilemma to which the Convention was exposed. By agreeing to the clause, it would revolt the Quakers, the Methodists, and many others in the States having no slaves. On the other hand, two States might be lost to the Union. Let us then, he said, try the chance of a commitment.

---

1. In this passage, which delegates supported and which opposed the clause as it stood?

2. What economic argument is Colonel Pinckney making?

3. What dilemma do the delegates face at this point?

Source 2

Exports from the American Colonies, 1768–1772

The commodities produced by the new nation did not differ substantially from those of the colonial period, so the numbers shown in the chart below paint the same general picture that the framers would have had in mind in 1787. One change, however, was that cotton, not a major export during colonial days, rose in importance. In fact, it became a commodity around which much of both the southern and northern economies revolved. Growing cotton, tobacco, indigo, and rice was backbreaking work and the South relied on enslaved labor to do that work.

Average Annual Value of Commodity Exports, 1768–1772 (in pounds sterling)				
Commodity	New England	Mid-Atlantic	Upper South	Lower South
Tobacco			756,128	
Indigo				111,864
Rice				305,533
Deerskins				37,093
Grains & grain products	19,902	379,380	199,485	13,152
Livestock, beef, pork	89,953	20,033		12,930
Wood products	65,271	29,348	22,484	
Iron		27,669	29,191	
Whale products	62,103			25,764
Fish	152,555			

Source: Excerpted from John McCusker and Russell Menard (1985). *The Economy of British America, 1607-1789.* Chapel Hill, NC: University of North Carolina Press

1. According to this chart, what are the South's main exports?

2. What are the main exports of the North?

3. Are the northern or the southern states more likely to use this data during the debate over Article 7, Section 4? Explain. What factors would this type of argument fail to take into consideration?

Source 3

Speech by James Iredell at the North Carolina Ratifying Convention, July 1788

After the Constitution was completed, the states held conventions to decide whether to ratify it. James Iredell, Sr., was a state judge, state attorney general, and later, a United States Supreme Court justice. The excerpt below is from a speech he made about Article 7, Section 4, which was included in the final document.

Mr. Chairman, I rise to express sentiments similar to those of the gentleman from Craven [a county in North Carolina]. For my part, were it practicable to put an end to the importation of slaves immediately, it would give me the greatest pleasure, for it certainly is a trade utterly inconsistent with the rights of humanity, and under which great cruelties have been exercised. When the entire abolition of slavery takes place, it will be an event which must be pleasing to every generous mind, and every friend of human nature; but we often wish for things which are not attainable. It was the wish of a great majority of the Convention to put an end to the trade immediately, but the states of South Carolina and Georgia would not agree to it. Consider then what would be the difference between our present situation in this respect, if we do not agree to the Constitution, and what it will be if we do agree to it. If we do not agree to it, do we remedy the evil? No, Sir, we do not. For if the Constitution be not adopted, it will be in the power of every state to continue it forever. They may or may not abolish it at their discretion. But if we adopt the Constitution the trade must cease after twenty years if Congress declare so, whether particular states please so or not; surely then we gain by it. This was the utmost that could be obtained. I heartily wish more could have been done. But as it is, this government is nobly distinguished above others by that very provision. Where is there another country in which such a restriction prevails? We therefore, Sir, set an example of humanity, by providing for the abolition of this inhuman traffic, though at a distant period. I hope therefore that this part of the Constitution will not be condemned, because it has not stipulated for what was impracticable to obtain.

1. Is Mr. Iredell in favor of or opposed to altering Article 7, Section 4 to allow Congress to ban the importation of enslaved people?

2. What reasons does Mr. Iredell give to convince his fellow delegates to support the Constitution?

3. Which delegate quoted in Source 1 holds a view most similar to Mr. Iredell's? Explain.

Source 4

William Rotch was a New England Quaker and shipping merchant. In this excerpt from his letter to a prominent Rhode Island industrialist, he expresses his position on the new Constitution. In the second excerpt, Charles Pinckney explains to the South Carolina House of Representatives why the southern states agreed to the addition to Art. 7, Sec. 4.

Letter from William Rotch, Sr., to Moses Brown, November 1787

. . . thou queries how friends [a name for members of the Quaker religion] can be active in establishing the new form of Government, which so much favors Slavery; alas in this point I must refer thee to some advocate for it, as to my own part my heart has been often pained since the publication of the doings of the Convention; and much disappointed I am as I had entertained some hope that so many wise men, would have formed some System of Government, founded on equity and justice, that thereby it might have acquired some strength and energy and that it might be on such a basis that we as a [Quaker] Society might lend our aid in establishing it so far as it tended to peace and morality; . . . it is evident to me it is founded on Slavery and that is on Blood. . . .

Excerpt from a Speech by Charles C. Pinckney, January 1788

It was alleged, by some of the members who opposed an unlimited importation, that slaves increased the weakness of any state who admitted them; that they were a dangerous species of property, which an invading enemy could easily turn against ourselves and the neighboring states; . . . . "Show some period," said the members from the Eastern States, "when it may be in our power to put a stop, if we please, to the importation of this weakness, and we will endeavor, for your convenience, to restrain the religious and political prejudices of our people on this subject." The Middle States and Virginia made us no such proposition; they were for an immediate and total prohibition. . . . [A] committee of the states was appointed in order to accommodate this matter, and, after a great deal of difficulty, it was settled on the footing recited in the Constitution.

---

1. Is William Rotch, Sr., in favor of or opposed to the proposed Constitution?

2. Which of these excerpts backs up the argument made by Mr. Randolph in Source 1? Explain.

3. How does Pinckney explain the reasons that South Carolina agreed to the addition to Art. 7, Sec. 4?

Lesson 1 The New Government Finds Its Way

CLOSE READING

Creating a New Government

1. **Identify Supporting Details** What important precedents did George Washington set as the first president? Take notes on this as you read this lesson.

Addressing the Nation's Debt

2. **Summarize** How did Hamilton's plan redistribute the wealth in the United States? Explain.

3. **Draw Conclusions** Why was it important for the United States government to suppress the Whiskey Rebellion?

Political Divisions Lead to Two Parties

4. **Compare and Contrast** Use the graphic organizer below to take notes about the similarities and differences between the Federalists and the Democratic Republicans. Include information about who made up each party, who led each party, what economic activities each party supported, and each party's attitude toward the federal government.

Federalists	Democratic Republicans

Domestic and Foreign Affairs

5. Draw Conclusions Why did the British help the American Indians fight against the United States?

6. Explain Arguments Explain why the Democratic Republicans were more likely to support the French Revolution, while the Federalists tended to oppose it.

7. Draw Inferences Why did the Jay Treaty of 1794 cause arguments in Congress?

Foreign Policy Affects Domestic Politics

8. Analyze Interactions Among Individuals, Events, and Ideas What events during John Adams's presidency led to Thomas Jefferson and the Democratic Republicans winning the presidency in the Election of 1800?

Lesson 2 Jefferson as President

CLOSE READING

A New Direction for American Government

1. **Compare and Contrast** Explain the difference between the ways Jefferson and Hamilton wanted to deal with the national debt. What were the goals of each leader?

2. **Analyze Interactions Among Individuals, Events, and Ideas** What Jeffersonian ideas are still alive in politics today?

John Marshall Shapes the Supreme Court

3. **Draw Inferences** What is the principle of judicial review and why was it necessary? Give an example.

A Growing Nation Looks Westward

4. **Summarize** Why did Jefferson choose to purchase the Louisiana Territory from Napoleon?

5. **Draw Conclusions** Why did Jefferson believe he had "done an act beyond the Constitution" by purchasing the Louisiana Territory?

Foreign Difficulties Challenge Jefferson

6. **Summarize** What was the U.S. "re-export" trade with France? Why did Britain oppose this trade?

7. **Identify Supporting Details** What were some of the dangers faced by American merchants in the 1790s and early 1800s? Give examples.

8. **Analyze Interactions Among Individuals, Events, and Ideas** What were the causes and effects of Jefferson's embargo with Britain? What did these effects reveal about the United States economy?

Lesson 3 The War of 1812

CLOSE READING

The Road to War

1. **Draw Inferences** Why did Congress fail in its attempts to force Britain and France to recognize American neutrality?

2. **Summarize** What were the main goals of Tecumseh and Tenskwatawa? Did they achieve these goals?

3. **Identify Supporting Details** Why did the War Hawks want to go to war against Britain? What did they hope to gain?

War With Britain

4. **Categorize** Use the graphic organizer below to list American successes and failures in the War of 1812. Include specific events.

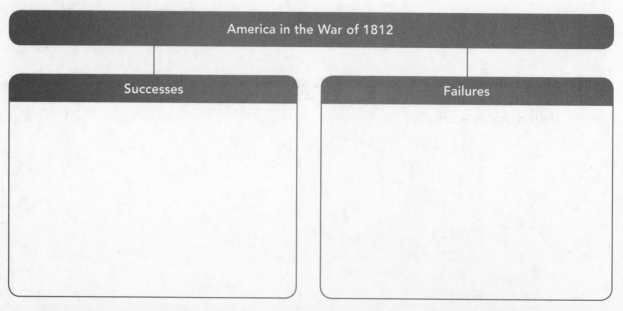

America in the War of 1812

Successes	Failures

5. Summarize What errors did the U.S. leaders make when planning the War of 1812?

The Impact of the War of 1812

6. Analyze Interactions Among Individuals, Ideas, and Events Why did the United States experience a surge of patriotism after the War of 1812?

7. Analyze Sequence What events led to the downfall of the Federalist Party?

8. Summarize Explain the geographic impact of the War of 1812.

Lesson 4 The Beginning of the Industrial Revolution

CLOSE READING

New Technology Revolutionizes Transportation

1. **Identify Cause and Effect** Why did transportation restrict economic growth in the United States before the 1800s?

2. **Summarize** How did the steamboat change transportation on the Mississippi River?

3. **Identify Supporting Details** How did the construction of the Eric Canal affect industry in the United States? Give at least two examples.

4. **Draw Inferences** What were the advantages of using railroads instead of canals to transport goods?

The Industrial Revolution

5. Draw Conclusions Why did Britain want to prevent the export of machines and knowledgeable employees?

6. Compare and Contrast How did the processes of making shoes and clothes change as a result of the Industrial Revolution?

Innovations in Industry and Agriculture

7. Draw Inferences What were the benefits of using interchangeable parts? Why did it take time for manufacturers to begin using interchangeable parts regularly?

8. Categorize What were some of the positive and negative consequences of the Industrial Revolution? Use the graphic organizer below to categorize your ideas.

Lesson 5 Differences Between North and South Grow

CLOSE READING

Industrialization Takes Hold in the North

1. **Analyze Interactions Among Individuals, Events, and Ideas** What effect did the War of 1812 have on northern industry?

2. **Identify Cause and Effect** How did the Tariff of 1816 affect the North and the South? Explain the positive and negative effects.

3. **Summarize** Why did the Industrial Revolution in the United States begin in the Northeast?

Industrialization Changes Northern Society

4. **Determine Central Ideas** Use the graphic organizer below to take notes about America's middle class, which expanded during the Industrial Revolution.

America's Middle Class	
Who They Were	
What They Did	Men: Women:
Where They Lived	

5. **Identify Cause and Effect** Describe how the immigrants who came to the United States in the 1840s and the 1850s affected the northern economy.

6. **Cite Evidence** What obstacles confronted the Irish and German immigrants who came to the United States during this time?

Agriculture Drives Southern Society

7. **Analyze Interactions Among Individuals, Events, and Ideas** What factors led to slavery becoming more deeply entrenched in the southern economy? Cite evidence from the text.

8. **Draw Inferences** How did the dominance of "King Cotton" prevent the spread of industrialization in the South?

Lesson 6 Nationalism Influences Policies

CLOSE READING

The Influence of Nationalism on Domestic Affairs

1. **Analyze Interactions Among Individuals, Events, and Ideas** What events led to the "era of good feelings"?

2. **Draw Inferences** What was the goal of economic nationalism?

3. **Explain Arguments** What were some of the arguments for and against establishing the second Bank of the United States? Use the graphic organizer below to organize your ideas.

Establishing a National Bank

For	Against

4. **Vocabulary: Determine Meaning** What is the "boom-and-bust" cycle and how does it work?

Nationalism Leads to American Expansion

5. **Analyze Interactions Among Individuals, Events, and Ideas** How did feelings of nationalism influence foreign policy?

6. **Determine Central Ideas** Summarize the main idea of the Monroe Doctrine. Explain why the United States instituted this policy.

Slavery and the Missouri Compromise

7. **Identify Cause and Effect** Explain the causes and effects of Denmark Vesey's planned uprising.

8. **Draw Conclusions** What was the purpose of the Missouri Compromise? Did it reach its goal?

Lesson 7 Jacksonian Democracy

CLOSE READING

Andrew Jackson Enters National Politics

1. **Identify Cause and Effect** How did the changes in voting rights affect American democracy?

2. **Draw Conclusions** What political strategies contributed to Andrew Jackson's success in the election of 1828?

American Indian Removal

3. **Draw Conclusions** What did the Trail of Tears show about many people's views about American Indians at the time?

The Debate Over Nullification

4. **Draw Inferences** Why were the southern states opposed to high tariffs?

Economic Change Leads to the Bank War

5. **Summarize** Explain why Andrew Jackson and many southerners opposed the creation of a national bank.

6. **Compare and Contrast** Use the graphic organizer below to show the differences between the beliefs of the Whigs and the Jacksonian Democrats. Also include information about the people who made up each party.

Whigs	Democrats

7. **Determine Central Ideas** How did Andrew Jackson exercise the power of the executive branch to a different extent than previous presidents? Cite evidence.

National Politics After Jackson

8. **Draw Inferences** What events and strategies contributed to the Whig victory in the Election of 1840?

PRIMARY SOURCE EXPLORATION

Should the United States Be Involved in Foreign Conflicts?

Introduction

In the early years of the United States, the new country's leaders debated how the country should deal with the conflict between its first ally, France, and its main trading partner, Britain. Should the United States side with one of the two combatants or remain uninvolved? The question whether to involve the United States in foreign conflicts has come up repeatedly in the country's history. The sources presented here offer contrasting perspectives on this question from different historical periods.

Document-Based Writing Activity

Analyze the following four sources and then use information from the documents and your knowledge of U.S. history to write an essay in which you

- Describe the issues and concerns around foreign military action that Americans have faced over time.
- Analyze the reasons why Americans have taken different positions on foreign military action.

Keep in mind that your essay should include an introduction, several paragraphs, and a conclusion. In the body of the essay, use evidence from at least three documents. Support your response with relevant facts, examples, and details. In developing your essay, be sure to keep these general definitions in mind:

- *Describe* means "to illustrate something in words or tell about it."
- *Analyze* means "to identify the different parts of a thing or situation in order to explain it in detail."

Source 1

"Pacificus III" and "Pacificus VII," Alexander Hamilton, 1793

In 1792, war broke out between France and Britain. Although the United States had a treaty of alliance with France, the U.S. government feared that the country would risk losing its independence if it challenged Britain—then the world's greatest power. President Washington issued the Proclamation of Neutrality in 1793. Alexander Hamilton defended this action in his Pacificus papers.

Pacificus No. III:

. . . With the possessions of Great Britain and Spain on both flanks, the numerous Indian tribes, under the influence and direction of those powers, along our whole interior frontier, with a long extended sea coast—with no [navy] of our own, and with the [navies] of all Europe against us, with no fortifications whatever and with a population not exceeding four millions—it is impossible to imagine a more unequal contest, than that in which we should be involved [if we were to fight on the side of France]; a contest from which we are dissuaded by the most [urgent] motives of self-preservation, as well as of interest. . . .

Pacificus No. VII:

. . . Spain, Holland, and England . . . are all commercial, maritime nations. It was to be expected that their attention would be . . . drawn towards the United States with [sensitivity], and even with jealousy. . . . . [Those countries] would naturally consider us as a power that might become their enemy. This they would have been the more [likely] to do, on account of those public demonstrations of attachment to the cause of France of which there has been so great a display. . . .

[Given] the probability of our being regarded with a suspicious and consequently an unfriendly eye by the powers at war with France; [given] the danger of [reckless acts] being committed by any of our citizens, which might occasion a [break with those powers]—the policy on the part of the government of removing all doubt as to its own [intention], and of deciding the condition of the United States in the view of the parties concerned became obvious and urgent. . . .

It is of much importance to the end of preserving peace, that the . . . powers [at war with one another] should be thoroughly convinced of the sincerity of our intentions to observe the neutrality we profess. . . .

1. In Pacificus III, how does Hamilton explain why he feels that the United States cannot afford to take sides in France's conflict with Britain?

2. According to Hamilton in Pacificus VII, why did the United States need to issue a proclamation of neutrality?

3. Why might foreign powers question the neutrality of the United States? Cite evidence from either source.

Source 2

The Rough Riders, Puck Magazine, July 27, 1898

This magazine cover shows future President Theodore Roosevelt leading the Rough Riders, a U.S. Army regiment, in Cuba during the Spanish-American War. It shows him trampling on Spanish soldiers and the Spanish flag, while other Spanish soldiers flee.

1. What attitude do this illustration and its caption take toward U.S. involvement in an overseas war against a foreign power?

THE ROUGH RIDERS.
THEY ARE ROUGH ON THE SPANIARDS, WHETHER THEY RIDE OR WALK.

2. How does the illustration portray the Rough Riders?

3. Consider that *Puck Magazine* wanted to sell as many copies as possible. What does this cover suggest about its American readers and their feelings about the Spanish-American War?

Source 3

Statement by the Student Nonviolent Coordinating Committee on the War in Vietnam, January 6, 1966

The Student Nonviolent Coordinating Committee (SNCC) was founded in 1960 by African American students involved in the U.S. civil rights movement. In the mid-1960s, the United States became increasingly involved in a war against communists in Vietnam. The U.S. government argued that it was fighting for the freedom of the Vietnamese. SNCC, like several other Civil Rights leaders and organizations, as well as many Americans of all races, opposed U.S. involvement in that war.

> The Student Nonviolent Coordinating Committee has a right and a responsibility to dissent with United States foreign policy on any issue when it sees fit. The Student Nonviolent Coordinating Committee now states its opposition to United States' involvement in Vietnam on these grounds:
>
> We believe the United States government has been deceptive in its claims of concern for the freedom of the Vietnamese people, just as the government has been deceptive in claiming concern for the freedom of colored people [an outdated term meaning Black people] in such other countries as the Dominican Republic, the Congo, South Africa, Rhodesia, and in the United States itself. . . .
>
> We ourselves have often been victim of violence and confinement [carried out] by United States governmental officials. We recall the numerous persons who have been murdered in the South because of their efforts to secure their civil and human rights, and whose murderers have been allowed to escape penalty for their crimes. . . .
>
> We are in sympathy with, and support, the men in this country who are unwilling to respond to a military draft which would compel them to contribute their lives to United States aggression in Vietnam in the name of the "freedom" we find so false in this country. . . .

1. Why are the members of SNCC suspicious of U.S. claims to be fighting for the freedom of the Vietnamese?

2. How do they describe the U.S. involvement in Vietnam?

3. What do you think is the main reason for SNCC's opposition to U.S. involvement in Vietnam?

Source 4

Address by Ambassador Susan Rice at the United States Institute of Peace, January 10, 2017

Susan Rice served as National Security Advisor under President Obama at a time when the United States had become the world's undisputed leading economic and military power. She gave this speech shortly before she left office and passed control over national security to the Trump administration. In it, she argues for the need for the United States to continue to play a role internationally for its own protection and for the protection of the "international order."

The global security landscape is as unsettled as any in recent memory. I could discuss this at length, but since time is short, I'll mention just three challenges.

First, Americans face a more diverse array of threats, from a more diverse range of sources, than ever. This includes everything from state actors such as Russia and North Korea to terrorists like [ISIS], often enabled by new technologies. And, it includes transnational [international] threats that can reach our shores—climate change, epidemics . . . , or the illicit flow of drugs and weapons.

Second, as a global leader and stakeholder, the United States faces the challenge of upholding an international order strained by rising tensions among major global and regional powers and deep governance challenges within them. Russia continues to threaten the global order—in Ukraine, in Syria, and through its efforts to interfere in democratic elections. China's assertiveness, most notably in the South China Sea, has tested whether the U.S.–China relationship will be defined by our differences or by what we can achieve cooperatively. Europe—buffeted by Brexit, economic uncertainty, a refugee and migrant crisis, and Russian aggression—needs American support now more than ever. Against this backdrop, as we've seen in the horrific tragedy in Syria, the Arab world will likely continue to struggle for stability—perhaps for a generation or more.

In the face of these challenges, it might be tempting to turn inward. Therein lies the United States' third strategic challenge. We must protect ourselves and the international order we helped build, without subordinating our values or abandoning the alliances, partnerships, and cooperation that have yielded unprecedented global prosperity and progress.

1. What response to challenges overseas does Ambassador Rice advocate for the United States? Cite evidence from the source.

2. Why does she feel that it is the responsibility of the United States to respond to those challenges?

3. What benefit does she see for the United States in responding to those challenges?

Lesson 1 Moving West

CLOSE READING

The Borderlands of Northern Mexico

1. Evaluate Explanations How did contact with Europeans reshape the lives of the Apaches?

2. Analyze Sequence How did the Apaches adapt to the changing culture of the West in the late 1700s and early 1800s?

3. Identify Cause and Effect Why did the Spanish have difficulty attracting settlers to California and Texas?

America Looks to the West

4. Identify Cause and Effect How did independence from Spain lead to Mexico's increasing economic dependence on the United States?

5. Analyze Interactions of Individuals and Ideas How did interaction between the United States and California develop?

Settling New Lands in the West

6. Categorize The Oregon Trail was full of difficulties and opportunities. Use the graphic organizer below to list what awaited settlers during this journey.

7. Make Predictions What conflicts can you imagine developing between American Indians and the ever-increasing flow of settlers in the West?

Lesson 2 Texas and the Mexican-American War

CLOSE READING

Texas Fights for Independence

1. **Evaluate Explanations** What was risky about Mexico's strategy in allowing Americans to settle in Texas?

2. **Summarize** Why did Santa Anna's style of governing alarm the Anglo-Texans?

3. **Draw Conclusions** What role did the issue of slavery play in the Texan Declaration of Independence?

The Expansion Debate

4. **Draw Inferences** Why did Northern representatives in Congress oppose President Jackson's desire to annex Texas?

5. **Cite Evidence** Why did northern Democrats feel betrayed by President Polk?

The Mexican-American War

6. **Evaluate Explanations** Why did the Mexicans refuse to recognize the U.S. annexation of Texas?

7. **Determine Central Ideas** What arguments did both Mexico and the United States present in order to justify the outbreak of war?

8. **Draw Inferences** Why did Whigs fear the U.S. annexation?

Lesson 3 The Nation Expands to the Pacific

CLOSE READING

The U.S. Gains Territory

1. **Draw Inferences** Why was Polk forced to accept the Treaty of Guadalupe Hidalgo?

2. **Determine Central Ideas** What changes in American politics did the war help reveal?

3. **Cite Evidence** What did the war reveal about northern public opinion?

4. **Identify Supporting Details** In what ways did the war have mixed consequences for the United States?

The California Gold Rush

5. **Identify Cause and Effect** How did the California Gold Rush affect the city of San Francisco? Use the graphic organizer below to keep track of causes and effects.

6. **Evaluate Explanations** Who gained the most wealth from the Gold Rush?

7. **Summarize** Why were mining camps so dangerous?

8. **Identify Supporting Details** In what ways did westward expansion threaten the unity of the United States?

Lesson 4 A Religious Awakening Sparks Reform

CLOSE READING

The Second Great Awakening/Religious Discrimination and Intolerance

1. **Summarize** Use the graphic organizer below to take notes on the important religious changes during the early 1800s. For each group, include information about the leader and if possible, the group's core beliefs.

Second Great Awakening

Mormons | Unitarians | AME | Evangelicals

2. **Determine Central Ideas** In what ways was the drive to reform all of society inspired by the Second Great Awakening?

Utopias and Transcendentalism

3. **Use Context Clues** What is a utopia? Explain how you used clues from the text to deepen your understanding of this word.

4. **Draw Inferences** What was the relationship between Transcendentalism and religious doctrine? Use evidence to support your ideas.

Public Education Reform

5. Summarize What improvements did reformers hope that the public school movement would bring to society?

6. Identify Main Idea How did Noah Webster's "spelling book" reflect the spirit of nationalism?

Social Reform Movements

7. Cite Evidence What were the goals of the prison reform movement? What were some of the problems with this movement?

8. Summarize Why was temperance such an important issue for many people?

Lesson 5 The Abolition Movement

CLOSE READING

Life as an Enslaved African American

1. **Identify Supporting Details** Find details from the text that support the idea that slavery was brutal and violated human rights.

2. **Cite Evidence** Describe at least three different ways enslaved people responded to their captivity. Give examples, if possible.

Free African Americans

3. **Analyze Interactions Among Individuals, Events, and Ideas** Explain the roots of the American Colonization Society, including why it was established.

The Antislavery Movement Grows

4. **Explain an Argument** Explain why some abolitionists argued for a gradual approach to emancipation, while others favored immediate emancipation for all enslaved people.

5. **Identify Cause and Effect** How did abolitionists publicize their arguments?

The Backlash Against Abolition

6. **Explain Arguments** Summarize some of the arguments slavery supporters used to justify slavery.

7. **Draw Inferences** Why did some Northerners support slavery?

8. **Categorize** Under each heading the graphic organizer below, show why slavery was such an important issue in the years leading up to the civil war.

Lesson 6 Women Work for Change

CLOSE READING

Women Fight for Reforms

1. **Identify Cause and Effect** In the chart below, explain why women became more politically active in the 1800s.

Reasons for Women's Activism in the 1800s

Second Great Awakening	Abolition Movement	Employment Opportunities

2. **Summarize** What legal and economic rights did women lack in the early 1800s?

Women Seek Expanded Rights

3. **Analyze Interactions Among Individuals, Ideas, and Events** What insight did the abolition movement give many women about the structure of power and gender roles in society?

4. **Compare and Contrast** How were the goals of the women's movement similar to the goals of the abolitionists? How were they different?

5. **Draw Inferences** Why were property rights such an important issue for the early women's movement?

The Seneca Falls Convention

6. **Cite Evidence** What were the immediate and long-term effects of the Seneca Falls Convention?

7. **Draw Inferences** Amelia Bloomer advocated for equality for women in all things, including the right to wear trousers instead of dresses. Why did she make a connection between clothing styles and women's rights?

PRIMARY SOURCE EXPLORATION

The Mexican-American War

Introduction

In the early 1800s, with American expansionists seeking new territory and Mexico in control of much of the land to the south and west of the United States, conflict between the two countries seemed inevitable. Congress voted to annex Texas in 1844, inflaming the long-standing border dispute between Texas and Mexico and leading to a war that would vastly increase the size of the United States.

Document-Based Writing Activity

Analyze the following four sources and then use information from the documents and your knowledge of American history to write an essay in which you

- Discuss the cause(s) of the war.
- Evaluate various perspectives on the war.

Keep in mind that your essay should include an introduction, several paragraphs, and a conclusion. In the body of the essay, use evidence from at least three documents. Support your response with relevant facts, examples, and details. In developing your essay, be sure to keep these general definitions in mind:

- *Discuss* means "to make observations about something using facts, reasoning, and argument; to present in some detail."
- *Evaluate* means "to examine and judge the significance, worth, or condition of; to determine the value of."

Source 1

President James K. Polk was an expansionist who had campaigned on acquiring Texas and Oregon territories. After the annexation of Texas, Polk sent American troops to occupy the borderland between Texas and Mexico. When a Mexican patrol killed American soldiers in May 1846, Polk rushed a declaration of war to Congress.

The existing state of the relations between the United States and Mexico renders it proper that I should bring the subject to the consideration of Congress. . . .

In my message at the commencement of the present session [of Congress] I informed you that upon the earnest appeal both of the Congress and convention of Texas I had ordered an efficient military force to take a position "between the Nueces and the Del Norte." This had become necessary to meet a threatened invasion of Texas by the Mexican forces, for which extensive military preparations had been made. The invasion was threatened solely because Texas had determined, in accordance with a solemn resolution of the Congress of the United States, to annex herself to our Union, and under these circumstances it was plainly our duty to extend our protection over her citizens and soil....

But no open act of hostility was committed until the 24th of April....A party of ... 63 men and officers were on the same day dispatched from the American camp up the Rio del Norte, on its left bank, to ascertain whether the Mexican troops had crossed or were preparing to cross the river, "became engaged with a large body of these troops, and after a short affair, in which some 16 were killed and wounded, appear to have been surrounded and compelled to surrender. . . ."

[N]ow, after reiterated menaces, Mexico has passed the boundary of the United States, has invaded our territory and shed American blood upon the American soil. She has proclaimed that hostilities have commenced, and that the two nations are now at war.

As war exists, and, notwithstanding all our efforts to avoid it, exists by the act of Mexico herself, ... I invoke the prompt action of Congress to recognize the existence of the war, and to place at the disposition of the Executive the means of prosecuting the war with vigor, and thus hastening the restoration of peace.

---

1. According to this account, why did Polk send U.S. troops to the region?

2. What is Polk asking Congress to do?

3. What does this account reveal about Polk's perspective on the war?

Source 2

"Matamoros Proclamation," General Francisco Mejia, March 18, 1846

General Francisco Mejia commanded the Mexican troops stationed on the south side of the Rio Grande awaiting American forces. Before U.S. troops arrived, Mejia issued this proclamation.

FELLOW-CITIZENS: The annexation of the department of Texas to the United States … does not yet satisfy the ambitious desires of the degenerate sons of Washington. The civilized world has already recognized in that act all the marks of injustice, iniquity, and the most scandalous violation of the rights of nations. Indelible is the stain which will for ever darken the character for virtue falsely attributed to the people of the United States; and posterity will regard with horror their perfidious conduct, and the immorality of the means employed by them to carry into effect that most degrading depredation…. To the United States, it has been reserved to put in practice dissimulation, fraud, and the basest treachery, in order to obtain possession, in the midst of peace, of the territory of a friendly nation, which generously relied upon the faith of promises and the solemnity of treaties. . . .

The cabinet of the United States does not, however, stop in its career of usurpation. Not only does it aspire to the possession of the department of Texas, but it covets also the regions on the left bank of the Rio Bravo…. What expectations, therefore, can the Mexican government have of treating with an enemy, who whilst endeavoring to lull us into security, by opening diplomatic negotiations, proceeds to occupy a territory which never could have been the object of the pending discussion? The limits of Texas are certain and recognized…

Fellow-countrymen: With an enemy which respects not its own laws, which shamelessly derides the very principles invoked by it previously, in order to excuse its ambitious views, we have no other resource than arms. We are fortunately always prepared to take them up with glory, in defense of our country; little do we regard the blood in our veins, when we are called on to shed it in vindication of our honor, to assure our nationality and independence. If to the torrent of devastation which threatens us it be necessary to oppose a dike of steel, our swords will form it; and on their sharp points will the enemy receive the fruits of his anticipated conquest….The flames of patriotism which burns in our hearts will receive new fuel from the odious presence of the conquerors…when we take up our march to oppose our naked breasts to the rifles of the hunters of the Mississippi.

1. According to this account, what is the United States seeking to do?

2. What is Mexico's only possible response, according to Mejia?

3. Who was the audience of this proclamation and what effect would reading it have on its readers?

Source 3

Speech in the United States House of Representatives, Abraham Lincoln, January 12, 1848

Abraham Lincoln, who represented Illinois in the U.S. House of Representatives from 1847 to 1849, repeatedly spoke out against the Mexican-American War. He urged President Polk to prove his claim that American soldiers had been attacked and killed on American soil; without this proof, Lincoln said, the war was unjustified.

The President, in his first message of May, 1846, declares that the soil was ours on which hostilities were commenced by Mexico; and he repeats that declaration, almost in the same language, in each successive annual message—thus showing that he esteems that point a highly essential one…. I propose to try to show that the whole of this…is, from beginning to end, the sheerest deception. . . .

[I]f any one should declare the President sent the army into the midst of a settlement of Mexican people, who had never submited, by consent or by force to the authority of Texas or of the United States, and that there … the first blood of the war was shed, there is not one word in all the President has said which would either admit or deny the declaration. In this strange omission chiefly consists the deception of the President's evidence…

If, as is probably true, Texas was exercising jurisdiction along the western bank of the Nueces, and Mexico was exercising it along the eastern bank of the Rio Grande, then neither region was the boundary; but the uninhabited country between the two was. . . .

Now, sir, for the purpose of obtaining the very best evidence as to whether Texas had actually carried her revolution to the place where the hostilities of the present war commenced, let the President … answer fully, fairly, and candidly…. But if he cannot, or will not do this… then I shall be fully convinced, of what I more than suspect already, that he is deeply conscious of being in the wrong; that he feels the blood of this war… is crying to Heaven against him; that he ordered General Taylor into the midst of a peaceful Mexican settlement, purposely to bring on a war;… trusting to escape scrutiny by fixing the public gaze upon the exceeding brightness of military glory—that attractive rainbow that rises in showers of blood.

---

1. According to Lincoln, what is "a highly essential" point in Polk's messages?

2. What does Lincoln mean by "that attractive rainbow that rises in showers of blood"?

3. How does Lincoln raise doubts about the cause of the war?

Source 4

"An Available Candidate" political cartoon, 1848

This 1848 political cartoon shows either Zachary Taylor or Winfield Scott, candidates for the Whig presidential nomination that year. Both were U.S. Army generals who led American troops in the Mexican-American War. Here, "available" refers to a combination of attractiveness and credibility.

AN AVAILABLE CANDIDATE.
THE ONE QUALIFICATION FOR A WHIG PRESIDENT.

For sale at 162 Spruce St. N.Y.

1. What does this cartoon show?

2. Did the creator of the cartoon support or oppose the Mexican-American War? How can you tell?

3. How might the artist respond to General Mejia's proclamation (Source 2)?

Lesson 1 Slavery Divides the Nation

CLOSE READING

Different Perspectives on the Issue of Slavery

1. **Summarize** Explain the views of abolitionists and how they were different from those of other northerners prior to the Civil War.

2. **Identify Cause and Effect** Why did some northern businessmen support slavery?

Slavery's Effect on the 1848 Election

3. **Vocabulary: Determine Meaning** Explain what popular sovereignty is and why it was appealing to both the Democrats and the Whigs in the Election of 1848.

The Compromise of 1850 Averts a Crisis

4. **Analyze Interactions Among Events** Explain how the California Gold Rush helped lead to the passage of the Fugitive Slave Act.

5. Categorize What aspects of the Compromise of 1850 were meant to appease the North? What parts were meant to appease the South? Use the graphic organizer below to categorize information.

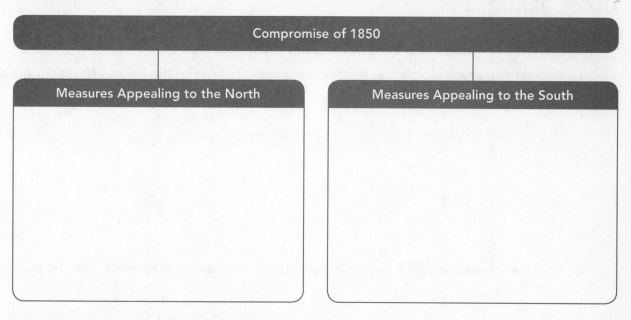

Northern Resistance to Slavery Increases

6. Compare and Contrast What effect did Congress expect the Fugitive Slave Act to have? What effect did it *actually* have?

7. Draw Conclusions Consider *Uncle Tom's Cabin* or *Blake*. How did this literary work affect or inspire different people?

Lesson 2 Violence Escalates

CLOSE READING

The Kansas-Nebraska Act and "Bleeding Kansas"

1. **Explain Arguments** Explain at least one argument in favor of the Kansas-Nebraska Act and one argument opposing this act.

2. **Analyze Interactions** What were the two sides in the conflict in Kansas? How did they try to win?

Regional Tension Affects National Politics

3. **Identify Cause and Effect** Explain what events led to the downfall of the Whig Party.

4. **Summarize** Describe the origins of the Republican Party.

Sectional Divisions Split the Country

5. Paraphrase Explain in your own words Frederick Douglass's reaction to the Dred Scott decision.

Lincoln and Douglas Debate Slavery

6. Summarize Use the graphic organizer below to show the positions of Abraham Lincoln and Stephen Douglas in the Lincoln-Douglas debates. Include nicknames and quotes as well as ideas that each candidate supported.

Lincoln	Douglas

The Raid on Harpers Ferry

7. Draw Conclusions Explain the effects of John Brown's raid on Harpers Ferry.

Lesson 3 The Civil War Begins

CLOSE READING

Sectional Politics in the Election of 1860

1. **Use Visual Information** What did the results of the Election of 1860 signify about the state of the Union? Use information from the election map to support your answer.

The Collapse of the Union

2. **Determine Author's Purpose** Explain Lincoln's purpose in his inaugural address in March 1861. What words and phrases from the address support your answer?

3. **Summarize** What happened at Fort Sumter and how did this contribute to the start of the Civil War?

Resources and Strategies

4. **Categorize** Use the graphic organizer below to list the strengths and weaknesses of the Union and the Confederacy in the Civil War.

	Union	Confederacy
Strengths		
Weaknesses		

5. **Compare and Contrast** Compare the initial military strategies of the Union and the Confederacy.

The First Year of the Civil War

6. **Draw Inferences** What did the North learn from the first Battle of Bull Run, also known as the Battle of Manassas?

A Stalemate in the East

7. **Summarize** What caused the stalemate in Virginia?

Lesson 4 African Americans and the War

CLOSE READING

Emancipation and the Civil War

1. **Draw Inferences** Why did Lincoln initially hesitate to emancipate enslaved African Americans?

2. **Identify Cause and Effect** What pressures, both inside and outside the United States, motivated Lincoln to issue the Emancipation Proclamation?

3. **Compare and Contrast** Why did Lincoln choose to announce the Emancipation Proclamation after the Battle of Antietam?

The Emancipation Proclamation

4. **Draw Inferences** The Emancipation Proclamation did not actually free a single enslaved person. Why did Lincoln choose to approach the issue in this way?

5. **Analyze Interactions Among Individuals, Ideas, and Events** How did the Emancipation Proclamation change the purpose of the Civil War for the North and the South?

African Americans Join the Fight

6. **Draw Inferences** How did the Union army show a conflicted attitude towards African American soldiers?

7. **Identify Supporting Details** Find details or examples that support this statement: African Americans in the South often found ways to passively or actively help the Union forces.

Lesson 5 Everyday Life During the War

CLOSE READING

Daily Life in the North

1. **Identify Cause and Effect** Why did some northerners resist the draft?

2. **Summarize** the ideas of the Peace Democrats and explain how Lincoln dealt with this faction.

Daily Life in the South

3. **Draw Conclusions** Explain why the Union blockade was so damaging to the Confederate government.

4. **Draw Inferences** What events and conditions caused resentment against the Confederate government and Jefferson Davis?

A Soldier's Life

5. Cite Evidence Describe the conditions for prisoners of war captured by the Confederate army. Cite evidence found in the text.

6. Identify Cause and Effect What factors contributed to the high death toll in the Civil War?

Women's Roles in Wartime

7. Summarize How did the Civil War contribute to the presence of women in the teaching and nursing professions?

Lesson 6 Key Civil War Battles

CLOSE READING

The Siege at Vicksburg

1. **Summarize** why Lincoln believed that Vicksburg was the key to a Union victory.

2. **Draw Conclusions** How did General Grant win the Battle of Vicksburg?

Confederate Advances Are Met at Gettysburg

3. **Sequence** Use this graphic organizer to take notes about key events that occurred during each day of the Battle of Gettysburg in July 1863.

Battle of Gettysburg

July 1	July 2	July 3

4. **Cite Evidence** Explain Abraham Lincoln's purpose in giving the Gettysburg Address. Cite quotes from the text to support your answer.

5. **Generate Explanations** What did President Lincoln mean in the Gettysburg Address when he said the country will have a "new birth of freedom"?

The Union's Total War

6. **Paraphrase** Why did General Sherman burn the city of Atlanta? Explain the reasons he gave in his letter to the mayor, James Calhoun.

7. **Draw Conclusions** Explain the effect of total war on Lincoln's reelection campaign. Then explain the effect of the total war strategy on the South.

Lesson 7 Impact of the Civil War

CLOSE READING

The War's End

1. Draw Conclusions Explain why the Siege of Petersburg was an important battle for both the Union and the Confederacy.

2. Summarize What were Lincoln's ideas about how to treat the Confederates after their surrender?

3. Analyze Interactions Among Individuals, Ideas, and Events What was John Wilkes Booth's goal in assassinating Lincoln? What effect did the assassination actually have?

Explaining the North's Victory

4. Vocabulary: Determine Meaning of Phrases What is a "war of attrition"? Why was the Civil War a war of attrition after a certain point?

5. Identify Central Ideas Why was the summer of 1863 so decisive for the Union?

The Costs of War

6. Compare and Contrast Explain the economic impact of the Civil War on the North and the South.

7. Draw Conclusions Identify and explain one long-term impact of the Civil War.

PRIMARY SOURCE EXPLORATION

Perspectives on Secession

Introduction

In 1860, Abraham Lincoln won election as President of the United States without winning any of the states of the South where slavery was legal. While Lincoln himself did not call for an end to slavery during his campaign, he wanted to stop its spread and many of his supporters did aim to abolish slavery. White southerners feared that, as President, Lincoln would ruin their economy and way of life by banning slavery. After Lincoln's election in late 1860, one southern state after another chose secession—or separation—from the United States. Many northerners believed that secession was wrong and unconstitutional. Within months, the dispute over secession and slavery led to the Civil War.

Document-Based Writing Activity

Analyze the following four sources and then use information from the documents and your knowledge of U.S. history to write an essay in which you

- Describe the point of view of each of the sources.
- Compare and explain the issues that drew different participants into the Civil War

Keep in mind that your essay should include an introduction, several paragraphs, and a conclusion. In the body of the essay, use evidence from all of the documents. Support your response with relevant facts, examples, and details. In developing your essay, be sure to keep these general definitions in mind:

- *Describe* means "to illustrate something in words or tell about it."
- *Compare* means "to examine things and see how they are similar."
- *Explain* means "to tell why something happened, give reasons for, or make understandable."

Source 1

A Declaration of the Immediate Causes which Induce and Justify the Secession of the State of Mississippi from the Federal Union, January 1861

After Lincoln's election in November 1860, many white southerners clamored for their states to leave the Union. Mississippi issued this declaration on January 9, 1861.

Our position is thoroughly identified with the institution of slavery-- the greatest material interest of the world. Its labor supplies the product [cotton and other cash crops] which constitutes by far the largest and most important portions of commerce of the earth. . . . These products have become necessities of the world, and a blow at slavery is a blow at commerce and civilization. That blow has been long aimed at the institution, and was at the point of reaching its consummation. There was no choice left us but submission to the mandates of abolition, or a dissolution of the Union. . . .

That we do not overstate the dangers to our institution [slavery], a reference to a few facts will sufficiently prove.

The hostility to this institution commenced before the adoption of the Constitution, and was manifested in the well-known Ordinance of 1787, in regard to the Northwestern Territory. [It banned slavery there.] . . .

It has grown until it denies the right of property in slaves . . .

It refuses the admission of new slave States into the Union, and seeks to extinguish it by confining it within its present limits, denying the power of expansion. . . .

It advocates negro [an outdated term meaning African American] equality, socially and politically . . .

It has given indubitable [clear] evidence of its design to ruin our agriculture . . . and to destroy our social system.

Utter subjugation awaits us in the Union, if we should consent longer to remain in it. It is not a matter of choice, but of necessity. We must either submit to degradation, and to the loss of property worth four billions of money, or we must secede from the Union framed by our fathers . . . . For far less cause than this, our fathers separated from the Crown of England.

Our decision is made. We follow their footsteps. We embrace the alternative of separation; and for the reasons here stated, we resolve to maintain our rights with the full consciousness of the justice of our course, and the undoubting belief of our ability to maintain it.

1. According to this declaration, what is Mississippi's main reason for seceding from the Union?

2. What historical example does the declaration claim to follow?

3. Why do you think white Mississippians saw Lincoln's election as such a threat?

Source 2

Memoirs of Mrs. Clay, of Alabama, Covering Social and Political Life in Washington and the South, 1853-66, Published 1904

Clement Clay was a senator from Alabama in early 1861, when most of the Southern slave states seceded from the United States. In her memoirs, Clement's wife Virginia recounts the day when her husband and other Southern senators announced their permanent departure from the U.S. Senate.

[It] was surely the saddest day of my life—January 21, 1861—when. . . I saw my husband take his portfolio under his arm and leave the United States Senate Chamber in company with other no less earnest Southern Senators. For weeks the pretense of amity [friendship] between parties had ceased, and social formalities no longer concealed the gaping chasm that divided them. When the members of each met, save for a glare of defiance or contempt, each ignored the other, or, if they spoke, it was by way of a taunt or a challenge. . . . and, when I heard the voice of my husband, steady and clear . . . declare in that Council Chamber:

"Mr. President, I rise to announce that the people of Alabama have adopted an ordinance whereby they withdraw from the Union, formed under a compact styled the United States, resume the powers delegated to it, and assume their separate station as a sovereign and independent people," it seemed as if the blood within me congealed [froze].

As each Senator, speaking for his State, concluded his solemn renunciation of allegiance to the United States, women grew hysterical and waved their handkerchiefs, encouraging them with cries of sympathy and admiration. Men wept and embraced each other mournfully. At times the murmurs among the onlookers grew so deep that the Sergeant-at-Arms was ordered to clear the galleries; and, as each speaker took up his portfolio and gravely left the Senate Chamber, sympathetic shouts rang from the assemblage above. Scarcely a member of that Senatorial body but was pale with the terrible significance of the hour. There was everywhere a feeling of suspense, as if, visibly, the pillars of the temple were being withdrawn and the great Government structure was tottering; nor was there a patriot on either side who did not deplore [be sorry or disapproving] and whiten before the evil that brooded so low over the nation.

1. What do you think Virginia Clay, as a white Southerner, meant by "the evil that brooded so low over the nation"?

2. How does she describe the atmosphere in the Senate?

3. What would explain why "the pretense of amity between parties had ceased," as Clay wrote?

Source 3

The Hercules of the Union, Slaying the Great Dragon of Secession, 1861

While some Northerners believed that the Southern states had a right to secede, many saw secession as a crime and secessionist leaders as criminals. In this cartoon, each of the dragon's heads represents a Southern secessionist leader, labeled on his neck with a crime. The man with the club about to strike the dragon is General Winfield Scott, commander of the Union Army at the time of the secession crisis.

THE HERCULES OF THE UNION,
SLAYING THE GREAT DRAGON OF SECESSION.

1. What does the cartoon suggest about the artist?

2. Why do you think the artist opposes secession? Cite evidence to support your view.

3. What does the cartoon suggest about the likely outcome of a conflict between the Union and the Confederacy?

Source 4

The Union and How to Save It, Frederick Douglass, February 1861

In the months before Abraham Lincoln took office as President in March 1861, most Southern states seceded. Many Northerners, hoping to save the Union without a violent conflict, called for compromise. In this essay, abolitionist Frederick Douglass rejects compromise and identifies slavery itself as the main threat to the Union.

[W]hat disturbs, divides and threatens to bring on civil war, and to break up and ruin this country, but slavery[?] Who but one morally blind can fail to see it; and who but a moral coward can hesitate to declare it[?] Fifteen States are bent upon the ascendency [dominance], and endless perpetuation of this system of immeasurable wickedness and numberless crimes, and are determined either to make it the law of the whole country, or destroy the Government. Against this inhuman and monstrous purpose are arraigned [called to judgment] the enlightenment of the age, checking and overthrowing tyranny, liberating the bondman [enslaved person] from his chains in all quarters of the globe, and extending constitutional liberty to long oppressed nationalities; against it are the instinctive sentiments of humanity . . . ; against it are the eternal laws of liberty, goodness, justice and progress . . .

Slavery is the disease, and its abolition in every part of the land is essential to the future quiet and security of the country. Any union which can possibly be patched up while slavery exists, must either completely demoralize the whole nation, or remain a heartless form, disguising, under the smiles of friendship, a vital, active and ever-increasing hate, sure to explode in violence. It is a matter of life and death. Slavery must be all in the Union, or it can be nothing. This is fully understood by the slaveholders of the cotton States and hence they can accept no compromise, no concession, no settlement that does not exalt [raise up] slavery above every other interest in the country. While there is a press unfettered [unchained], or a human tongue left free, the land will be filled with alarm and agitation. . . . [T]he country must remain a spectacle of anarchy, and be a byword and a hissing to a mocking earth, till this basis of eternal justice and liberty shall be the foundation of our Union.

1. Does Douglass see secession as the most important issue confronting the Union? Explain.

2. Why does Douglass believe that Southerners are unwilling to compromise?

3. Why does Douglass think that slavery must end for the Union to survive?

Lesson 1 Plans for Reconstruction Clash

CLOSE READING

The Challenges of Reconstruction

1. **Explain an Argument** Explain why some Northerners wanted to give the freed African Americans in the South land confiscated from or abandoned by plantation owners. Explain why Southerners opposed this policy.

2. **Identify Supporting Details** Identify three details that support the following main idea: the Civil War devastated the South.

3. **Summarize** What challenges did newly freed people face after emancipation?

Competing Reconstruction Plans

4. **Compare and Contrast** Use the graphic organizer below to compare and contrast how Lincoln and the Radical Republicans believed the South should be treated after the Civil War. Include information about the plans proposed by each.

Lincoln: *Ten Percent Plan*	Radical Republicans: *Wade-Davis Bill*

5. **Draw Conclusions** Why did Lincoln support the Freedmen's Bureau but oppose the Wade-Davis Bill?

The Johnson Presidency and Reconstruction

6. **Compare and Contrast** How were Johnson's views about Reconstruction different from Lincoln's?

7. **Summarize** How did Southerners limit the rights of freed African Americans? Give several examples.

Congress Passes a Plan for Reconstruction

8. **Identify Cause and Effect** Why were the Radical Republicans so powerful in the years following the Civil War?

Lesson 2 Reconstruction Changes the South

CLOSE READING

Republicans Dominate Government

1. **Compare and Contrast** Explain the similarities and differences between the scalawags and the carpetbaggers.

2. **Identify Cause and Effect** Why were many African Americans able to gain political power and positions immediately following the Civil War? Give at least two reasons from the text.

3. **Draw Inferences** Why did more African Americans gain legislative positions in the South than in the North?

Freed People Rebuild Their Lives

4. **Draw Conclusions** How was life different for freed African Americans after the Civil War? What aspects of life were similar?

5. **Analyze Interactions Among Individuals, Ideas, and Events** How did African Americans use educational institutions and churches to develop their communities after the Civil War?

Land Distribution in the South

6. **Compare and Contrast** Use the graphic organizer below to show the similarities and differences among the various ways of managing land in the South after the Civil War. Include information about how much autonomy the farmers had in each situation.

Sharecropping	Share-Tenancy	Tenant Farming

Changes in the South Spark Violence

7. **Draw Conclusions** What tactics were used by the Ku Klux Klan? What was the goal of this group?

8. **Paraphrase** Read the quotation by Isaiah Wears. What are his key points?

Lesson 3 Reconstruction's Impact

CLOSE READING

Reconstruction Comes to an End

1. **Draw Conclusions** How did the Slaughterhouse Cases and *United States* v. *Cruikshank* affect the scope of the Fourteenth Amendment?

2. **Identify Supporting Details** What techniques did the Democratic Party use to gain power in the South?

3. **Draw Inferences** What were the terms of the Compromise of 1877? Why did Southerners agree to it?

Reconstruction Leaves a Mixed Legacy

4. **Cite Evidence** Identify one way in which Reconstruction had benefited African Americans by the late 1870s. Then identify one way in which it fell short.

The South Restricts African American Rights

5. **Identify Supporting Details** Give two examples of how southern whites restricted the voting rights of African Americans in the years after the Civil War. Explain why these examples particularly impacted African Americans.

6. **Draw Inferences** What was the goal of the Jim Crow laws? Explain whether this goal was achieved.

African American Leaders Seek Reform

7. **Compare and Contrast** Use the graphic organizer below to compare and contrast the philosophies of Booker T. Washington and W.E.B. Du Bois.

Booker T. Washington	W.E.B. Du Bois

8. **Summarize** What was the main issue that Ida B. Wells focused on? Why was that issue important for attaining equal rights for African Americans?

PRIMARY SOURCE EXPLORATION

The Legacy of the Fifteenth Amendment

Introduction

On February 3, 1870, the Fifteenth Amendment, the last of the Reconstruction Amendments, was ratified. It expanded the right to vote to African American men by making it illegal to prevent people from voting based on their "race, color or previous condition of servitude." This right did not last for long. A period known as "Redemption" followed Reconstruction. Whites used violence, terror, and the legal system to end the political gains of African Americans in the South. In response, Black activists and Republicans who supported their cause began a new struggle to end voter discrimination.

Document-Based Writing Activity

Analyze the following four sources and then use information from the documents and your knowledge of American history to write an essay in which you

- Describe the impact of the political gains of African Americans during Reconstruction.
- Discuss the legacy of the Fifteenth Amendment. How were the voting rights of African Americans affected?

Keep in mind that your essay should include an introduction, several paragraphs, and a conclusion. In the body of the essay, use evidence from at least three documents. Support your response with relevant facts, examples, and details. In developing your essay, be sure to keep these general definitions in mind:

- *Describe* means "to illustrate something in words or tell about it."
- *Discuss* means "to make observations about something using facts, reasoning, and argument; to present in some detail."

Source 1

"Reconstruction Reassessed," by E.L. Godkin, *The Nation*, December 7, 1871

During Reconstruction, African Americans rose to positions of power across the South. This Republican magazine editor questioned both their ability and the speed with which they were given authority. His opinion reflects racist and condescending attitudes that were common among white people at the time, even among abolitionists like Godkin.

It is comparatively easy to reform the tariff or the civil service, or reduce the taxes, or return to specie payments, or civilize the Indians, or protect the immigrants, or get the overdue instalment [sic] from Venezuela, or bring Mexico to reason on that matter of "the free zone" but it is almost as hard to give order, peace, and security to the southern half of American society as to medicine to a mind diseased, or pluck the rooted sorrow from the brain. We do not need to tell any of our readers what the state of things in that region is. It is not simply that men suddenly raised from a condition of bestial servitude [cruel, inhuman slavery]… have been admitted to participation in the rights and responsibilities of free society; it is that they have been put in full and exclusive control of that most delicate and complicated piece of mechanism known as the government of a civilized State, with its debts, its credit, its system of taxes, its system of jurisprudence, its history, its traditions, its thousand knotty social and political problems…. [W]e gave them possession of the government, and deprived them of the aid of all the local capacity and experience in the management of it, thus offering the States as a prey to Northern adventures, and thus inflicting on the freedmen the very worst calamity which could befall a race… that is, familiarity, in the very first moments of enfranchisement, with the processes of a corrupt administration, carried on by gangs of depraved vagabonds, in which the public money was stolen, the public faith made an article of traffic, the legislature openly corrupted. . . . We do not hesitate to say that a better mode of debauching the freedmen… could hardly have been hit on had the North had such an object deliberately in view.

1. What criticisms does Godkin make of southern governments led by African Americans? What language does he use that indicates a lack of respect for freed people?

2. Consider what you know about how southern African Americans used their new rights. How might an African American politician from the time have responded to Godkin's critique?

3. How might opinions like Godkin's have presented an obstacle to African Americans trying to preserve their rights as Reconstruction ended?

Source 2

Testimony of Milton Claiborne Nicholas, United States v. R.B. Foster

In 1870, Milton Claiborne Nicholas prepared to vote for the first time. The ballots were cast in writing. Nicholas could not read or write. He would have to depend on someone to assist him in casting his vote. During the process, Nicholas felt his vote was wrongly place. He decided to complain. He appealed to the Commissioners Court of the Eastern District of Virginia in Richmond. This is his story.

> When I went in at the door, Mr. Foster asked me to let him see my ticket. I let him take it in his hand—Foster told me I was ignorant [and] did not know what I was talking. [He] had been trying to persuade me how to vote. Foster then handed my ticket to the clerk and told the clerk to take off Mr. Parsons name and put on Mr. Vaughns name. Parsons was the Republican Candidate for sheriff[.] I I said. Mr. Foster please don't alter the ticket I want to vote the full Radical ticket; let it go straight just as it is. The clerk changed the ticket. I then reached for the ticket but he would not hand it to me—but gave it to Strong one of the Judges [and] told him to put it in the box—[and] the ticket was put in—I never had possession of any ticket after it was changed. I am 31 years old [and] I lived in Gouchland county all my live [and] was registered in the precinct when I offered to vote… If I had gotten possession of the ticket after it was changed I would not have voted it.

1. What problems did Nicolas encounter when entering the voting facility?

2. Why do you think Foster changed Nicholas's choice for sheriff?

3. One newspaper article of the time reported that the "Commissioner, after a careful examination decided to dismiss the case." Discuss the significance of this lawsuit.

Source 3

Smith v. Allwright, 1944

When S.S. Allwright, a white election official denied Lonnie E. Smith, a Black man, the right to vote in the 1940 Texas Democratic primary, the case was fought all the way to the Supreme Court.

MR. JUSTICE REED delivered the opinion of the Court.

This writ of certiorari brings here for review a claim for damages in the sum of $5,000 on the part of the petitioner, a Negro [African American] citizen of the 48th precinct of Harris County, Texas, for the refusal of respondents, election and associate election judges, respectively, of that precinct, to give petitioner a ballot in the primary election of July 27, 1940, for the nomination of Democratic candidates for the United States Senate and House of Representatives, and Governor and other state officers. The refusal is alleged to have been solely because of the race and color of the proposed voter.

The actions of respondents are said to violate §§ 31 and 43 of Title 8. . . of the United States Code. . . in that petitioner was deprived of rights secured by. . . .Article 1 and the Fourteenth, Fifteenth, and Seventeenth Amendments to the United States Constitution. The suit was filed in the District Court of the United States for the Southern District of Texas which had jurisdiction.

The District Court denied the relief sought, and the Circuit Court of Appeals quite properly affirmed its action on the authority of *Grovey v. Townsend*. We granted the petition. . . to resolve a claimed inconsistency between the decision in the *Grovey* case and that of the *United States v. Classic*.

The State of Texas by its Constitution and statutes provides that every person, if certain other requirements are met which are not here in issue, qualified by residence in the district or county "shall be deemed a qualified elector."

---

1. According to the suit, the denial of Smith's rights violated which amendments?

2. How do you know that this is not the first case of this kind to appear before the court?

3. How do you think this decision changed voter participation in Texas at that time?

Source 4

Shelby County v. Holder and the memory of civil rights progress, Abigail Perkiss, November 25, 2013.

Nearly a century after Reconstruction, the passage of the Voting Rights Act of 1965 gave force to the Fifteenth Amendment, using federal power to protect African Americans' right to vote. However, debates surrounding the law continued, resulting in a key Supreme Court ruling in 2013.

Earlier this month, on November 5, 2013, American voters went to the polls for the first time since the U.S. Supreme Court issued its decision in *Shelby County v. Holder*, striking down a key provision of the 1965 Voting Rights Act. . . .

The act applied a nationwide prohibition against the denial or abridgment of the right to vote based on former Jim Crow laws. And it also prohibited state and local governments with a history of discriminatory voting from implementing changes without first going through a "preclearance" federal oversight process. In essence, it decreed that states and municipalities with a track record of racial injustice would be required to get permission from the federal government before changing their voting policies and guidelines. This could be an expensive and labor-intensive process, but it was one of the key mechanisms for enforcing the law. . . .

In 2006, [Congress] extended the law for another 25 years. During congressional debates that year, some argued the preclearance requirement constituted an overreach of federal power and an undue burden on Southern states that, they claimed, have long since abandoned their discriminatory patterns.

These conversations – in Congress and around the nation more broadly – culminated in 2012 when the Supreme Court agreed to hear *Shelby County v. Holder*. In the case, Shelby County, Alabama sued the US Attorney General, seeking for these preclearance requirements to be declared unconstitutional. The petitioner argued that the preclearance procedure was excessively expensive for small Southern counties and also that it was an overreach of federal oversight on state and local governments.

In a 5-4 ruling, one of the final decisions announced in the 2013 season, the Court held that this preclearance clause is, indeed, unconstitutional.

The decision has already immediate practical consequences. Texas announced shortly after the Roberts opinion was released that a previously blocked voter identification law would go into effect immediately, and that redistricting maps there would no longer need federal approval. Pennsylvania, as well, will rely on the decision to justify the implementation of their ID requirements.

---

1. What was the purpose of "preclearance" in the Voting Rights Act of 1965?

2. Do you think the issue of states' rights was involved? Explain.

3. How did this decision change voting practices?

Lesson 1 Innovation Boosts Growth

CLOSE READING

American Industry Grows

1. **Identify Cause and Effect** As you read "American Industry Grows," use this graphic organizer to record factors that encouraged the growth of industry in the United States (the causes of industrialization) as well as industrialization's effects.

2. **Analyze Interactions Among Events** What technological innovation changed the oil industry in the mid-1800s? How did this change encourage the growth of industry in general?

Innovation Drives Economic Development

3. **Identify Supporting Details** How did railroads and factories cause a "spiral of growth" during the Industrial Revolution? Identify details that explain and support this idea.

Industrialization and the New South

4. Compare and Contrast As you read "Industrialization and the New South," use this graphic organizer to compare and contrast industrialization and agriculture in the old and new South.

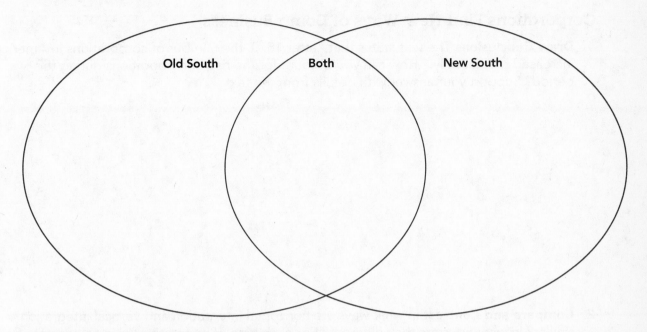

Old South   Both   New South

The Effects of Industrialization

5. Identify Cause and Effect During the Industrial Revolution, many people moved away from farms and into cities. What caused this migration? What effects did moving into the city have on the people who chose to do this?

6. Draw Inferences What were some benefits of industrialization to the United States? What were some problems that it caused? Use details from the text as well as your own ideas and experience to list and explain at least two significant "pluses" and two possible "minuses" of industrialization.

Lesson 2 Big Business Rises

CLOSE READING

Corporations Find New Ways of Doing Business

1. **Draw Conclusions** The text states that "after 1870, the number of corporations in America increased dramatically." How can you account for the rise of corporations during this period? Support your answer with details from the text.

2. **Compare and Contrast** In what ways are horizontal integration and vertical integration similar? In what ways are they different? For each type of integration, give an example from the text of a corporation that used the strategy, and explain how the corporation used it.

The Pros and Cons of Big Business

3. **Assess an Argument** What arguments did critics of big business use to argue that so-called "robber barons" were harming the economy?

4. **Vocabulary: Determine Meaning** Read the first two paragraphs of "The Causes and Effects of Social Darwinism." What do you think Social Darwinism is? How was Social Darwinism used to justify prejudice against minorities? Use evidence from the text to support your answer.

The Changing Relationship Between Government and Business

5. **Cite Evidence** The United States has a history of tension between business and government. Give at least two examples of this conflict from the text and explain them.

6. **Identify Supporting Details** What were the goals of the Sherman Antitrust Act? What was its unintended consequence?

Lesson 3 The Organized Labor Movement

CLOSE READING

Workers Endure Difficulties

1. **Summarize** what it was like to work in a sweatshop in the late 1800s. Include details from the text.

2. **Identify Cause and Effect** Why did many children hold factory jobs at the end of the 1800s? How did working at young ages affect these children?

3. **Draw Conclusions** What were the benefits of company towns and company stores to the businesses that ran them? Cite evidence to support your conclusions.

The Growth of Labor Unions

4. **Identify Arguments** What did socialists in the 1800s advocate?

5. **Compare and Contrast** How were the goals and actions of the Knights of Labor similar to those of the American Federation of Laborers (AFL)? How were the goals and membership different?

Labor Unions Lead Protests

6. **Identify Cause and Effect** Why did public opinion begin to turn against unions after the Haymarket demonstration in Illinois and the Homestead Strike in Pennsylvania? Support your answer with evidence from the text.

7. **Explain an Argument** What argument did the railroads use in court to persuade the government to end the Pullman workers' strike? Explain the argument.

8. **Summarize** how the outcome of the Pullman Strike affected trade unions over the next few decades.

Lesson 4 The New Immigrants

CLOSE READING

New Immigrants Seek Better Lives

1. **Compare and Contrast** How were the "new" immigrants that came to the United States between 1870 and 1900 different from earlier immigrants? Cite specific evidence from the text.

2. **Categorize** As you read "Causes of Immigration," use this graphic organizer to take notes about the "push factors" and the "pull factors." First, define *push factor* and *pull factor* in the appropriate box. Then record examples of push and pull factors listed in the text.

Push Factors	Pull Factors
A "push factor" is . . .	A "pull factor" is . . .

Optimism and the Immigrant Experience

3. **Compare Authors' Points of View** Compare the excerpts from the two primary source quotations in this section. How do the authors' points of view differ? What do they suggest about differences in the ways Asian and European immigrants were treated?

Social Issues Affecting Immigrants

4. **Summarize** What kinds of discrimination did immigrants face in the new country?

5. **Cite Evidence** The text states that many immigrants and established Americans alike viewed the United States as a melting pot. From what you have read in "Social Issues Affecting Immigrants," do you agree that the United States was a melting pot early in the 1900s? Cite evidence from the text to support your answer.

Immigrants Affect American Society

6. **Identify Supporting Details** In "Immigrants Affect American Society," the text argues that immigrants transformed American society. Cite and explain an example that supports this central idea.

7. **Analyze Interactions** How did the "new" immigrants affect the politics of unionization, and what motivated them to do so?

Lesson 5 A Nation of Cities

CLOSE READING

Americans Migrate to Cities

1. **Determine Central Ideas** As you work through each reading in this lesson, use this graphic organizer to note the central ideas.

2. **Paraphrase** As the text points out, a historian once noted that the United States was born on the farm and moved to the city. What does this statement mean? Put it in your own words. What evidence does the text give to support this idea?

3. **Draw Conclusions** How did urbanization contribute to the growth of the middle class?

4. **Identify Cause and Effect** What "push factors" drove farmers to leave their farms and move to the city? What "pull factors" might have attracted farmers to city life?

Technology Improves City Life

5. Analyze Interactions What innovations helped make the construction of skyscrapers possible? How did skyscrapers, in turn, help fuel urban growth?

6. Draw Conclusions Which invention or innovation from this period do you think had the most important impact on daily life in U.S. cities? Support your answer with evidence.

Urban Living Creates Social Issues

7. Summarize what tenement life was like. Use details from the text to support your description.

8. Identify Supporting Details Cities in the late 1800s struggled with sanitation and safety. Give an example of an improvement that people made to make city life healthier or safer. Use details from the text to explain your example.

Lesson 6 New Ways of Life

CLOSE READING

Free Enterprise Improves Life

1. **Vocabulary: Use Context Clues** What is "conspicuous consumerism"? Look for clues throughout "Free Enterprise Improves Life." Then use the clues to define the phrase.

2. **Analyze Interactions** During the Gilded Age, the standard of living rose in the United States. What technological developments contributed to this rise in the standard of living?

A Mass Culture Develops

3. **Identify Supporting Details** The turn of the century brought many "firsts," including advances in entertainment, education, and the arts. Keep track of those innovations in the graphic organizer below as you read "A Mass Culture Develops" and "A Boom in Popular Entertainment."

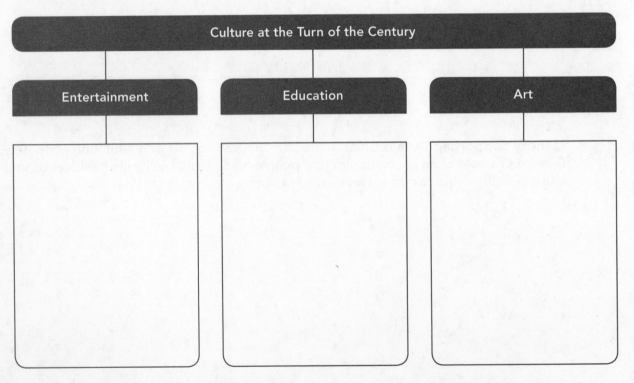

Culture at the Turn of the Century

Entertainment	Education	Art

4. **Analyze Interactions** How did the needs of business and industry influence public education in the United States? Cite specific examples from the text.

5. **Summarize** the educational opportunities available to women and African Americans at the turn of the century.

A Boom in Popular Entertainment

6. **Draw Conclusions** Several major cities hosted exhibitions of new technology and entertainment during the Gilded Age. How did exhibitions like these reflect the times?

7. **Compare and Contrast** Which forms of entertainment popular during the Gilded Age are still popular today? What does their enduring popularity suggest about entertainment during that time?

PRIMARY SOURCE EXPLORATION

Immigrant Experiences

Introduction

In the late 1800s and early 1900s, millions of immigrants came to the United States. While each immigrant had his or her own story, many shared certain common experiences. Other experiences were unique to immigrants from different backgrounds, or those who moved to particular areas in the United States. What might a Chinese immigrant who opened a restaurant in New York City have in common with an Irish immigrant who became a farmer in Nebraska? What experiences might set the two apart?

Document-Based Writing Activity

Analyze the following four sources and then use information from the documents and your knowledge of American history to write an essay in which you

- Compare and contrast the experiences of immigrants from different ethnic or cultural backgrounds.
- Compare and contrast the experiences of immigrants who settled in rural and urban areas in the United States.

Keep in mind that your essay should include an introduction, several paragraphs, and a conclusion. In the body of the essay, use evidence from at least three documents. Support your response with relevant facts, examples, and details. In developing your essay, be sure to keep this general definitions in mind:

- *Compare and contrast* means "to examine things and see how they are both similar <u>and</u> different."

Source 1

Guide to the United States for the Immigrant Italian, translated by John Foster Carr, 1911

The language barrier was a problem for many immigrants. While some were able to live comfortably in immigrant neighborhoods where their native language was widely spoken, many immigrants needed to quickly learn English to find work and settle down.

Learn English

English is absolutely indispensable to the workman. He needs it in order to find work. He needs it to take directions and have his work explained. He needs it unless he is willing to work for the smallest wages with no hope of increase. He needs it when he is in difficulties to avoid interested helpers. He needs it to protect himself without requiring the help of the law. He needs it to understand words of warning and keep out of danger, for every year hundreds of Italians are hurt or killed in America, because they do not understand the shouts of warning, or do not know how to read danger signals, when a few English words might have saved their lives. You cannot be in America a single day without understanding the necessity of speaking the same language that all other men in America speak.

How Can You Learn English Quickly:
. . . The eye can be of use too. The signs on store windows and offices, on wagons and posters, will all help to identify strange words to you. Buy one of the cheap illustrated American papers every night (they cost so little, one cent a copy) and try to study out the news. After you have made a little progress, buy the weekly papers that are illustrated. Buy a ten-cent magazine and study it.

. . . The best help you can get will be from those who speak English. Make friends with Americans. If possible, for the first six months go and live among Americans. Find an American boarding house, if you can; for this will do much more for you than give you the chance of learning English. You will be learning many important things about the United States, as well as the customs and ways of American family life, and you will be learning to understand the ideas and ideals of our Republic.

1. Of the reasons listed why a workman needs to learn English, which do you think is the most important? Explain your answer.

2. Identify three techniques for learning English listed in this guide.

3. This guide is aimed at Italian immigrants. Would guides like these be useful to other groups of immigrants? Why or why not?

Source 2

"The Biography of Chinaman," Lee Chew, *Independent,* 1903

Chinese immigrant Lee Chew wrote a short autobiography for the *Independent* magazine after two decades in the United States. He thrived in America despite widespread prejudice against Chinese immigrants. The term "Chinaman" used in the title of this piece is a racial slur that was widely used at the time of this publication and is considered highly offensive today.

It was twenty years ago when I came to this country, and I worked for two years as a servant, getting at the last $35 a month. I sent money home to comfort my parents, but tho I dressed well and lived well and had pleasure, going quite often to the Chinese theater and to dinner parties in Chinatown, I saved $50 in the first six months, $90 in the second, $120 in the third and $150 in the fourth So I had $410 at the end of two years, and I was now ready to start in business.

When I first opened a laundry it was in company with a partner, who had been in the business for some years. … We had to put up with many insults and some frauds, as men would come in and claim parcels that did not belong to them, saying they had lost their tickets, and would fight if they did not get what they asked for. Sometimes we were taken before Magistrates and fined for losing shirts that we had never seen. On the other hand, we were making money, and even after sending home $3 a week I was able to save about $15. When the railroad construction gang moved on we went with them. The men were rough and prejudiced against us, but not more so than in the big Eastern cities. It is only lately in New York that the Chinese have been able to discontinue putting wire screens in front of their windows, and at the present time the street boys are still breaking the windows of Chinese laundries all over the city, while the police seem to think it a joke….

The reason why so many Chinese go into the laundry business in this country is because it requires little capital and is one of the few opportunities that are open. Men of other nationalities who are jealous of the Chinese, because he is a more faithful worker than one of their people, have raised such a great outcry about Chinese cheap labor that they have shut him out of working on farms or in factories or building railroads or making streets or digging sewers. He cannot practice any trade, and his opportunities to do business are limited to his own countrymen. So he opens a laundry when he quits domestic service.

The treatment of the Chinese in this country is all wrong and mean. It is persisted in merely because China is not a fighting nation. The Americans would not dare to treat Germans, English, Italians or even Japanese as they treat the Chinese, because if they did there would be a war.

1. Did Lee Chew succeed during this time working in Chinatown? How can you tell?

2. Why did Chinese immigrants go into the laundry business, according to this excerpt?

3. How does Lee Chew compare the Chinese immigrant experience to that of other immigrant groups?

Source 3

Tenement Life Photographs, Lewis Hine

Many immigrants to the United States settled in cities. Living conditions in densely-packed immigrant neighborhoods could be poor, and life was not easy for new arrivals. The photographer Lewis Hine captured images of these two families living in crowded tenement apartments.

A family of eight squeezes around the table to share a sparse meal in their tenement home.

A woman, two children, and a pet cat gather in a cramped bedroom. Why might pans be placed around the room?

1. What challenges of urban immigrant life do these photos depict?

2. How do the families seem to be coping with their living conditions? What are they doing that might make life more pleasant?

3. How might the lives of these families be different if they were living in a rural area? How might they be similar?

Source 4

Excerpts from an interview with Mrs. John Donnelly, November 1938

Irish immigrant Margaret Donnelly recalls her experience living on a Nebraska farm as a child during the 1870s.

I was born in Balley Matz, Ireland in 1861. My folks came to America in my early childhood, settling at Fairbury, Illinois. During the Chicago fire, it was in the fall of 1871, we came to Sutton, Nebraska and filed on a homestead, seven miles southwest of the town. The country was all open prairie.

Our nearest neighbor lived 1 1/2 miles distant. We had built a sod house and broke a small patch of land with our oxen and planted corn and garden stuff. We had plenty of rain and everything grew. We got corn and lots of vegetables. We made a cellar and stored our vegetables in it for the winter. We usually had corn bread on our table. Prairie chickens were plentiful. They provided us with meat. Of course the men had to go out and shoot them. But there were so many that they always got some. Our vegetables lasted till the next summer. We had no papers to read in those days. The neighbors would all come together at one place this Sunday and then at another the next until they had made the round. Then they would do this over and over again. This way we got all the news. . . .

At first there was no school in the neighborhood. After a few years, we built a small school building. We had three months of school during the year. Reading, writing, arithmetic and geography was taught. Most of the pupils learned to read write and figure enough to get them through the world at that time. We didn't need much of the foolishness taught in schools nowadays. We were Catholics. At first we had no services. Later when a Missionary came to Sutton, we went to church there. The trip was not fast, because our oxen took their time. In the winter we burned corn stalks, tumbling weeds and ox chips to keep warm. Later on we always had some coal in the winter. The people were pretty sensible in the early days.

---

1. What kind of dwelling did the author's family live in?

2. Did the family in this excerpt struggle to find enough to eat? How did the area they lived in help or hurt them?

3. What challenges did rural immigrants like Mrs. John Donnelly face that urban immigrants likely did not? Explain your answer.

Lesson 1 American Indians Under Pressure

CLOSE READING

Cultures Forced to Adapt

1. **Analyze Sequence** As you read this lesson, use this timeline to record important dates and events in the struggle between the American Indians and white settlers. Connect each event to the timeline at the right place (for example, connect an event that took place in 1855 to a spot in between 1850 and 1860).

2. **Summarize** how the U.S. government's policy toward American Indians changed between the early 1800s and the 1850s. What caused this change?

Settlers and American Indians Collide

3. **Identify Cause and Effect** What triggered the Sand Creek Massacre? How did Plains Indians respond to the attack?

4. **Paraphrase** the statements that Chief Piapot made about the Canadian government's treatment of American Indians. Could the same criticisms of the treatment of American Indians be made against the U.S. government? Support your answer with evidence from the text.

The Indian Wars Conclude

5. **Compare and Contrast** the struggles of the Sioux and the Nez Percés. In what ways were they similar? In what ways were they different?

6. **Draw Conclusions** Why do you think that the United States government found the Ghost Dance revival threatening?

The Government Encourages Assimilation

7. **Determine Central Ideas** In your opinion, what was the most significant effect of the Indian Wars on American Indians? Explain your thinking.

Lesson 2 The West is Transformed

CLOSE READING

Mining and the Growth of Railroads

1. **Identify Key Steps in a Process** Mining stimulated the development of new towns, some of which became well established. Identify the key steps in this process, and briefly explain how each step led to the next.

2. **Determine Central Ideas** What were the main benefits to the nation of a transcontinental railroad?

The Cattle Industry Boom

3. **Compare and Contrast** cattle ranching before and after the invention of barbed wire.

Farmers Settle the Plains

4. **Categorize** As you read "Farmers Settle the Plains," use this graphic organizer to keep track of the advantages and disadvantages to people of settling on the Great Plains.

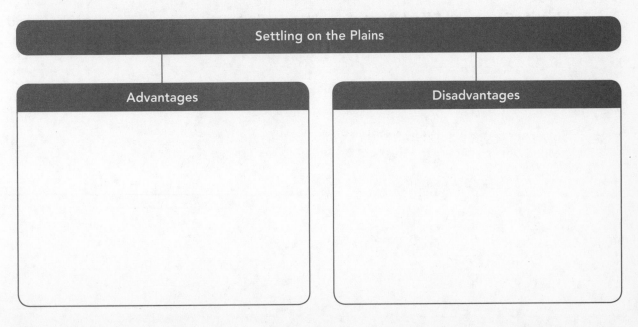

Settling on the Plains

Advantages	Disadvantages

Minorities Encounter Difficulties

5. **Cite Evidence** that Chinese immigrants and Mexican Americans were discriminated against in the West. How did these groups respond to the discrimination?

6. **Determine Central Ideas** Throughout this lesson, what central idea is conveyed about minorities and the parts they played in the settling of the American West?

Struggles and Change Across the West

7. **Identify Cause and Effect** What caused tension between miners, farmers, ranchers, and sheepherders that settled in the West? Give examples of situations that created tension.

Lesson 3 Corruption Plagues the Nation

CLOSE READING

Political Power Proves Difficult to Keep

1. **Identify Cause and Effect** During the Gilded Age, no political party gained power for any length of time. How did this balance affect Congress's productivity? Why did it affect Congress in this way?

2. **Identify Supporting Details** Why did the public begin to lose faith in the government during the Gilded Age? Support your ideas with evidence from the text.

Growth of Political Machines and Corruption

3. **Categorize** What were benefits and drawbacks of the spoils system? Complete the graphic organizer below as you read "Growth of Political Machines and Corruption."

Spoils System

Benefits	Drawbacks

4. **Analyze Interactions** Why did public support for civil service reform grow after the assassination of President James Garfield?

Economic Policy Challenges Continue

5. **Explain an Argument** Why did Republicans support a high tariff? Why did Democrats oppose a high tariff? Explain each party's argument.

6. **Draw Inferences** During the Gilded Age, farmers supported the minting of silver because it would increase the money supply and cause inflation. What does farmers' desire for inflation suggest about the prices they were being paid for their crops? Explain your reasoning.

Lesson 4 Farm Issues and Populism

CLOSE READING

Farmers Face Economic Difficulty

1. **Analyze Interactions** As you read the text for this lesson, use this graphic organizer to keep track of important ideas. In the first column, note economic problems that farmers faced. In the second column, note causes of the economic problems. In the third column, note actions that farmers took to solve the problems.

Problems	Causes	Farmers' Responses

2. **Paraphrase** the quotation from the farmers' newspaper by putting it in your own words. Based on evidence in the text, do you think that the author's point of view is justified? Explain.

Farmers Seek Change Through Alliances

3. **Summarize** the goals of the Farmers' Alliance. Did the Alliance achieve those goals? Cite textual evidence to explain why or why not.

The Beginnings of Populism

4. **Vocabulary: Use Context Clues** Read the first paragraph of "The Beginnings of Populism." What do you think the term *grassroots* means? What context clues helped you figure out this definition?

5. **Determine Central Ideas** Explain the strategy of the Populist Party. To what groups did it try to appeal and why?

Populism's Declining Influence

6. **Analyze Style and Rhetoric** Analyze how William Jennings Bryan used language to appeal to populists in his "Cross of Gold" speech. What words, phrases, or expressions do you think would appeal the most to the audience and why?

7. **Identify Cause and Effect** What factors contributed to the downfall of the Populist Party? Use information from both "The Beginnings of Populism" and "Populism's Declining Influence" to identify cause and effect.

PRIMARY SOURCE EXPLORATION

Impact of Westward Movement and Settlement on American Indians

Introduction

Since colonial times, European settlers and their American descendants had been gradually taking over American Indian lands. The pace increased as the United States expanded westward after the Civil War. The impact on Plains Indians took many forms — loss of livelihood, loss of land, loss of life, and loss of freedom. But, despite strong resistance, all of it was devastating to the American Indians' way of life.

Document-Based Writing Activity

Analyze the following four sources and then use information from the documents and your knowledge of American history to write an essay in which you

- Describe different ways that westward movement and settlement affected Plains Indians.
- Discuss the goals and impact of the U.S. government's Indian policies.

Keep in mind that your essay should include an introduction, several paragraphs, and a conclusion. In the body of the essay, use evidence from at least three documents. Support your response with relevant facts, examples, and details. In developing your essay, be sure to keep these general definitions in mind:

- *Describe* means "to illustrate something in words or tell about it."
- *Discuss* means "to make observations about something using facts, reasoning, and argument; to present in some detail."

Source 1

"Buffalo Hunting," Harper's Weekly, December 14, 1867

The herds of bison that once roamed the Great Plains were vital to the Plains Indians' way of life. But settlers moving westward saw them differently. This article and illustration appeared in the popular magazine *Harper's Weekly, A Journal of Civilization*.

Our engraving represents a sport that is peculiarly American. At this season of the year the herds of buffalo are moving southward, to reach the canyons which contain the grass they exist upon during the winter. Nearly every railroad train which leaves or arrives at Fort Hays on the Kansas Pacific Railroad has its race with these herds of buffalo; and a most interesting and exciting scene is the result. The train is "slowed" to a rate of speed about equal to that of the herd; the passengers get out fire-arms which are provided for the defense of the train against the Indians, and open from

This engraving shows well-dressed westbound travelers shooting at bison on the Great Plains.

the windows and platforms of the cars a fire that resembles a brisk skirmish. Frequently a young bull will turn at bay for a moment. His exhibition of courage is generally his death-warrant, for the whole fire of the train is turned upon him, either killing him or some member of the herd in his immediate vicinity.

When the "hunt" is over the buffaloes which have been killed are secured, and the choice parts placed in the baggage-car, which is at once crowded by passengers, each of whom feels convinced and is ready to assert that his was the shot that brought down the game. Ladies who are passengers on the trains frequently enjoy the sport, and invariably claim all the game as the result of their prowess with the rifle.

---

1. How do the train passengers view the buffalo herds?

2. Do you think the author of this article approved of this hunt? How can you tell?

3. The Plains Indians were buffalo hunters themselves. How do you think they would view the hunt described here?

Source 2

Speech on Treatment of Indians on Reservations, Susette La Flesche, 1881

Susette La Flesche belonged to a prosperous family of mixed French and Indian background. She was educated first at a reservation mission school in Nebraska, and later at a girls' school in New Jersey. In 1881, she accompanied the Omaha chief Standing Bear on a lecture tour, where she gave the speech reported here.

The chairman of the Board of Indian Commissioners says: "Reservations are used for Indians very much as nurseries are used for children, as safe enclosures for the weak and defenseless." Does he call them safe enclosures because in them the Indians are powerless to help themselves when robbed? I know that hundreds of horses have been stolen from my tribe, the Omahas, and they cannot do a single thing to recover their property, punish the thieves or stop the robbery. A horse was stolen from my father last spring. He knows who stole the horse, and he knows the white man who has the horse now. He asked the agent to help him get it back. The agent was as powerless as he was, and told me that the best way to do would be for my father to steal it back. Two Crows, one of the most intelligent men I ever knew whether white or red, and who has been the lifetime friend of our family, has had stolen from him during the last three years, fourteen working horses. He said that as fast as he could collect money enough together to buy new ones to work his farm with they were stolen from him....

As to our lives being protected, a white man can kill an Indian any time and they are powerless to redress the wrong. If they retaliate and kill a white man in revenge for the deed, the troops are sent and war made on the tribe. . . .

As to the traders – just think of eleven hundred people being compelled by law to buy of and sell to only one man. It is a fine of a $1,000 dollars and six months' imprisonment for a white man to buy of or sell to an Indian. How can the Indian grow rich when he is compelled to sell all his wheat to a trader at forty cents a bushel, when wheat buyers outside of a reserve are willing to pay ninety cents a bushel; and the trader does not pay for our wheat or corn in money, but in calico or whatever else he had in his store.

1. According to La Flesche, what power did the U.S. government agent at the reservation have to protect the Indians from theft?

2. What evidence does she offer to show that Indians are not treated equally under the law?

3. What economic restrictions do Indians farmers labor under? What is the result?

Source 3

President Benjamin Harrison on Indian Policy, State of the Union Address, December 3, 1889

Benjamin Harrison served one term as U.S. President, from 1889-1893. The year before Harrison was elected, Congress had passed the Dawes Act. Its goal was to break up traditional Indian land holdings and encourage American Indians to become private farmers. Here, Harrison evaluates the effects of that policy.

Substantial progress has been made in the education of the children of school age and in the allotment of lands to adult Indians. It is to be regretted that the policy of breaking up the tribal relation and of dealing with the Indian as an individual did not appear earlier in our legislation. Large reservations held in common and the maintenance of the authority of the chiefs and headmen have deprived the individual of every incentive to the exercise of thrift, and the annuity [annual payment earlier given to Indians] has contributed an affirmative impulse toward a state of confirmed pauperism.

Our treaty stipulations should be observed with fidelity and our legislation should be highly considerate of the best interests of an ignorant and helpless people. The reservations are now generally surrounded by white settlements. We can no longer push the Indian back into the wilderness, and it remains only by every suitable agency to push him upward into the estate of a self-supporting and responsible citizen. For the adult the first step is to locate him upon a farm, and for the child to place him in a school.

School attendance should be promoted by every moral agency, and those failing should be compelled. The national schools for Indians have been very successful and should be multiplied, and as far as possible should be so organized and conducted as to facilitate the transfer of the schools to the States or Territories in which they are located when the Indians in a neighborhood have accepted citizenship and have become otherwise fitted for such a transfer. This condition of things will be attained slowly, but it will be hastened by keeping it in mind; and in the meantime that cooperation between the Government and the mission schools which has wrought much good should be cordially and impartially maintained.

1. Does Harrison think the Dawes Act has been successful? Explain.

2. According to Harrison, how would the policies he describes benefit Indians? Do you agree or disagree?

3. What bias can you identify in Harrison's statements? Give two examples.

Source 4

Black Elk Speaks: Being the Life Story of a Holy Man of the Oglala Sioux, as told through John G. Neihardt, 1932

Black Elk was a cousin of the Sioux military leader Crazy Horse. He had been present at the fighting at Little Big Horn and witnessed the massacre at Wounded Knee. In 1932, when he was 69 years old, Black Elk told an interviewer about the final surrender of the Sioux in the aftermath of Wounded Knee.

We wanted a much bigger war-party so that we could meet the soldiers and get revenge. But this was hard, because the people were not all of the same mind, and they were hungry and cold. We had a meeting there, and were all ready to go out with more warriors, when Afraid-of-His-Horses came over from Pine Ridge to make peace with Red Cloud, who was with us there.

Our party wanted to go out and fight anyway, but Red Cloud made a speech to us something like this: "Brothers, this is a very hard winter. The women and children are starving and freezing. If this were summer, I would say to keep on fighting to the end. But we cannot do this. We must think of the women and children and that it is very bad for them. So we must make peace, and I will see that nobody is hurt by the soldiers."

The people agreed to this, for it was true. So we broke camp next day and went down from the O-ona-gazhee to Pine Ridge, and many, many Lakotas were already there. Also, there were many, many soldiers. They stood in two lines with their guns held in front of them as we went through to where we camped.

And so it was all over.

I did not know then how much was ended. When I look back now from this high hill of my old age, I can still see the butchered women and children lying heaped and scattered all along the crooked gulch as plain as when I saw them with eyes still young. And I can see that something else died there in the bloody mud, and was buried in the blizzard. A people's dream died there. It was a beautiful dream.

---

1. What was the chief goal of Black Elk and his party before Red Cloud's speech?

2. What were the main reasons the Sioux finally decided to surrender?

3. According to Black Elk, what was the ultimate result of the events he describes?

Lesson 1 Progressives Drive Reform

CLOSE READING

The Progressive Era Begins

1. **Summarize** What problems did the Progressives see with life in the 1890s? How did they approach these problems?

2. **Compare and Contrast** Progressivism was related to the Populist movement in the late 1800s. Complete a Venn diagram that shows how the two movements were similar and different. Include information about the people who participated in each movement and the ideals driving each movement.

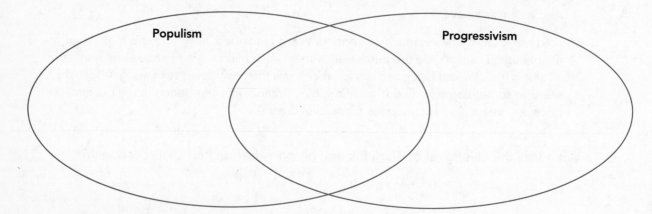

Populism   Progressivism

The Impact of Muckrakers

3. **Analyze Style and Rhetoric** Based on the excerpt from *McClure's Magazine*, "Corruption and Reform in St. Louis," how would you describe Lincoln Steffens's writing style? What language seems especially provocative?

Reformers Impact Society

4. Cite Evidence What role did Christianity play in the Progressive movement? Cite evidence for your answer.

5. Draw Inferences What issues with factories did the Triangle Shirtwaist Factory Fire bring to light? Explain.

Progressive Reforms Impact Government

6. Identify Cause and Effect Why did Galveston, Texas, replace its city government with a commission? What were the effects of the commission government?

7. Paraphrase Explain in your own words why some people opposed direct election of senators, a reform that was passed in the Seventeenth Amendment.

Lesson 2 Women Gain Rights

CLOSE READING

Expanding Opportunities for Women

1. **Identify Cause and Effect** What trends led to the rise of the suffrage movement in the 1890s?

2. **Analyze Interactions** Florence Kelley and the National Consumers League put special labels on good that were produced under "fair, safe, and healthy working conditions." Give an example of how this is still important to consumers today.

3. **Draw Inferences** How was the women's suffrage movement connected to the temperance movement?

4. **Cite Evidence** Why did Margaret Sanger view birth control as a women's rights issue? Look for evidence throughout the text to explain.

5. **Identify Supporting Details** What rights did Ida B. Wells work for in the African American community?

Women Seek Equal Political Rights

6. **Analyze Style and Rhetoric** In the *Ladies Home Journal* excerpt, how did Jane Addams use language to persuade women of the importance of women's suffrage?

7. **Analyze Interactions of People and Events** How did the women's suffrage movement benefit from linking itself with Progressivism?

8. **Compare and Contrast** Compare the approaches of Carrie Chapman Catt and NAWSA and Alice Paul and the NWP toward women's suffrage. Both claimed credit for the Nineteenth Amendment. Who do you think deserved more credit, and why?

Lesson 3 Striving for Equality

CLOSE READING

Minorities Face Challenges in the Progressive Era

1. **Determine Central Ideas** Throughout this lesson, what central idea is conveyed about Progressivism?

2. **Cite Evidence** The Progressives wanted to assimilate many immigrant groups. Give two examples of this from the text.

African Americans Promote Civil Rights

3. **Evaluate Explanations** There was some tension between the approaches of Booker T. Washington and W.E.B. Du Bois in how to approach African American civil rights. What approach was more convincing, and why? Use details from the text to support your answer.

4. **Vocabulary: Use Context Clues** Describe the "peonage" mentioned in the NAACP's goals. Why were African Americans forced into peonage?

5. **Summarize** How did the NAACP advocate for the civil rights of African Americans? Give specific examples.

Protecting Rights for Ethnic and Religious Minorities

6. **Identify Supporting Details** Many ethnic or religious minorities helped each other by creating services in their own communities. Give an example of how a minority built up a community through social services.

7. **Draw Conclusions** The text states that the Dawes Act of 1887 and the American Indian Citizenship Act of 1924 were both designed to help Americanize the American Indians. Explain the negative effects of these laws.

8. **Compare and Contrast** Compare the struggles the American Indians and the Asian Americans went through to gain voting rights and own land.

Lesson 4 Reformers in the White House

CLOSE READING

Roosevelt Changes the Relationship Between Government and Business

1. **Paraphrase** Describe Theodore Roosevelt's Square Deal and explain in your own words what he meant when he compared his policy to a hand of cards.

2. **Summarize** Use the graphic organizer below to take notes on the positive and negative effects of the creation of the Interstate Commerce Commission.

Interstate Commerce Commission

Positive Effects

Negative Effects

Managing the Environment

3. **Analyze Interactions Among People, Events, and Ideas** Are Gifford Pinchot's ideas about "rational use" of natural resources still applicable today? Explain why or why not.

4. Draw Inferences Explain why building and managing dams and reservoirs out West might have negative consequences as well as positive ones.

A New Direction in Presidential Politics

5. Compare Authors' Points of View Compare the excerpt from Wilson's "The New Freedom" with Roosevelt's explanation of the Square Deal. How was Wilson's rhetoric different?

Wilson Endorses Further Regulation

6. Explain an Argument Why did Wilson choose to cut tariffs and introduce the graduated income tax? Why did many Congressmen and business leaders oppose the graduated income tax?

The Progressives' Legacy

7. Determine Central Ideas What was the most significant contribution of the Progressive presidents, Theodore Roosevelt and Woodrow Wilson? What was their impact on the United States?

Lesson 5 American Influence Grows

CLOSE READING

America on the World Stage

1. **Summarize** Explain the connection between Manifest Destiny and Christianity.

2. **Identify Cause and Effect** How did European imperialism affect the foreign policy of the United States?

3. **Paraphrase** What did historian Frederick Jackson Turner mean when he argued for a "safety valve"?

America Begins to Expand

4. **Summarize** Why did the Japanese close off their ports to the rest of the world prior to Perry's voyage? Why did they agree to trade with the United States?

5. **Categorize** Use the graphic organizer below to take notes on the advantages and disadvantages of William Seward's purchase of Alaska.

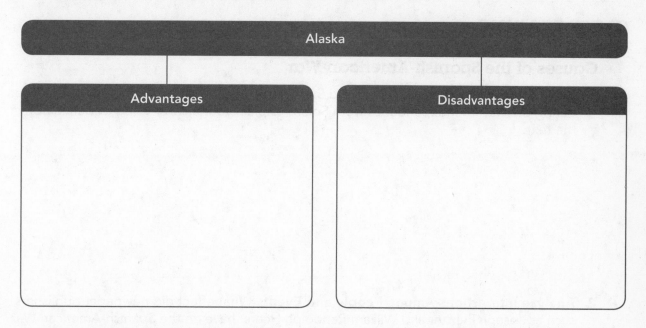

6. **Draw Conclusions** During the 1860s, the United States occupied the Midway Islands and acquired Alaska. Why did America expand into these new territories? How were the reasons for acquiring both territories similar?

The Acquisition of Hawaii

7. **Analyze Sequence** What were the most important events in the process of the annexation of Hawaii by the United States?

8. **Explain an Argument** Why did the planters want a new Hawaiian constitution? Why did Queen Liliuokalani oppose the new constitution?

Lesson 6 The Spanish-American War

CLOSE READING

Causes of the Spanish-American War

1. **Draw Conclusions** Why did the United States have an interest in what happened in Cuba during the war for independence from Spain? Explain your answer using evidence from the text.

2. **Analyze Interactions Among People and Events** What effect did newpaper publishers such as Joseph Pulitzer and William Randolph Hearst have on the Spanish-American War?

American Forces Defeat the Spanish

3. **Analyze Sequence** Why was the United States able to defeat the Spanish in the Philippines so easily? What other events led to this victory?

4. **Cite Evidence** Secretary of State John Hay called the Spanish-American War a "splendid little war." Based on the information presented in the text, do you agree? Explain your answer, citing evidence in the text to support your ideas.

The War as a Turning Point

5. Draw Inferences After the United States victory in the Spanish-American War, President McKinley said America had no choice but to "take them all, and to educate the Filipinos, and uplift and civilize . . . them." What does this quote reveal about McKinley and his attitude toward the Filipinos?

6. Explain an Argument Explain why some Americans were opposed to taking control of the Philippines.

Effects of U.S. Expansionism in the Philippines

7. Draw Inferences A newspaper article quoted in the text explains that the United States wanted the Philippines but not the Filipinos. Explain why.

8. Draw Conclusions Why did the Filipino leader Emilio Aguinaldo fight with the United States against Spain? Why did he later fight against the United States?

9. Cite Evidence What actions by the United States showed negative attitudes toward the Filipinos? Give examples from the text.

Lesson 7 The United States Emerges as a World Power

CLOSE READING

U.S. Trade and Intervention in China

1. **Draw Conclusions** During the Age of Imperialism, what were the benefits to having "spheres of influence" in China and other countries rather than colonies?

2. **Draw Inferences** What was the Boxer Rebellion? Why did the United States get involved in it?

Roosevelt Works With Japan

3. **Identify Supporting Details** Describe Theodore Roosevelt's foreign policy goals and actions in Asia. Give at least two examples of his actions and draw conclusions about those actions.

American Foreign Policy in Latin America

4. **Compare and Contrast** Use the Venn diagram below to compare and contrast the Foraker Act for Puerto Rico and the Platt Amendment for Cuba.

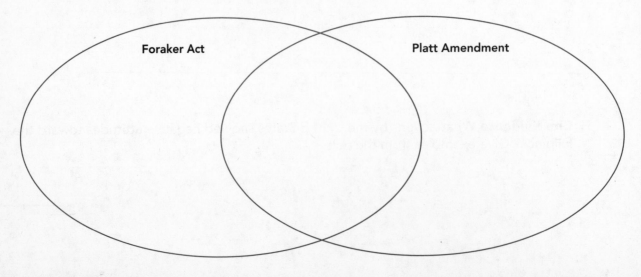

Foraker Act

Platt Amendment

"Big Stick" Diplomacy

5. **Paraphrase** Explain what Theodore Roosevelt meant when he promoted "big stick" diplomacy.

6. **Analyze Sequence** What precedent did the Roosevelt Corollary set about the U.S. international presence?

7. **Compare and Contrast** Explain how "dollar diplomacy" differed from "big stick" diplomacy.

Wilson's "Moral Diplomacy"

8. **Cite Evidence** How did U.S. imperialism impact the formation of governments in Latin America in the early 1900s? Cite evidence from any of the texts in this lesson to support your answer.

9. **Summarize** Why did Wilson consider the intervention in Mexico to be an example of "moral diplomacy"?

PRIMARY SOURCE EXPLORATION

U.S. Imperialism in the Philippines

Introduction

During the Spanish-American War, the Filipino nationalist leader Emilio Aguinaldo and American forces were fighting on the same side. Their shared goal was to end Spanish rule in the Philippines. However, after the war, their goals differed. Aguinaldo declared the Philippines an independent republic and was inaugurated as its first president. The United States, on the other hand, decided to keep control of the islands. Thus began a three-year war between the United States and the Philippines. Aguinaldo's guerrilla forces were finally defeated in 1902. But Aguinaldo lived long enough to see his dream come true when the Philippines became an independent nation in 1946.

Document-Based Writing Activity

Analyze the following four sources and then use information from the documents and your knowledge of American history to write an essay in which you

- Evaluate U.S. policy in the Philippines after the Spanish-American War.
- Describe how Americans disagreed on the subject of imperialism in the Philippines.

Keep in mind that your essay should include an introduction, several paragraphs, and a conclusion. In the body of the essay, use evidence from at least three documents. Support your response with relevant facts, examples, and details. In developing your essay, be sure to keep these general definitions in mind:

- *Evaluate* means "to examine and judge the significance, worth, or condition of; to determine the value of."
- *Describe* means "to illustrate something in words or tell about it."

Source 1

Benevolent Assimilation proclamation, President William McKinley, December 21, 1898

After the Spanish-American War, the United States purchased the Philippines from Spain. But Americans were unsure what to do with their new territory. President McKinley announced his decision in December 1898. He called his policy "benevolent assimilation."

[A]s a result of the victories of American arms, the future control, disposition, and government of the Philippine Islands are ceded to the United States...

It will be the duty of the commander of the forces of occupation to announce and proclaim in the most public manner that we come not as invaders or conquerors, but as friends, to protect the natives in their homes, in their employments, and in their personal and religious rights.

All persons who, either by active aid or by honest submission, co-operate with the Government of the United States to give effect to these beneficent purposes will receive the reward of its support and protection. All others will be brought within the lawful rule we have assumed, with firmness if need be, but without severity, so far as possible....

The taxes and duties heretofore payable by the inhabitants to the late government become payable to the authorities of the United States unless it be seen fit to substitute for them other reasonable rates or modes of contribution to the expenses of government, whether general or local. If private property be taken for military use, it shall be paid for when possible in cash, at a fair valuation, and when payment in cash is not practicable, receipts are to be given. . . ."

Finally, it should be the earnest wish and paramount aim of the military administration to win the confidence, respect, and affection of the inhabitants of the Philippines by assuring them in every possible way that full measure of individual rights and liberties which is the heritage of free peoples, and by proving to them that the mission of the United States is one of BENEVOLENT ASSIMILATION substituting the mild sway of justice and right for arbitrary rule. In the fulfilment of this high mission, supporting the temperate administration of affairs for the greatest good of the governed, there must be sedulously maintained the strong arm of authority, to repress disturbance and to overcome all obstacles to the bestowal of the blessings of good and stable government upon the people of the Philippine Islands under the free flag of the United States.

1. What promises does McKinley make to the Filipino people? What does he expect from them?

2. What threats does McKinley imply in his proclamation?

3. How do you think McKinley would define the term "benevolent assimilation?"

Source 2

General Elwell Otis served as U.S. military commander and Governor-General of the Philippines. Otis sent a copy of McKinley's "benevolent assimilation" declaration to Filipino nationalist leader Emilio Aguinaldo. Aguinaldo responded by issuing this declaration to the people of the Filipinos.

General Otis is proclaimed Military Governor of the Philippines and I protest a thousand times and with all the force in my soul against such pretension. I solemnly declare that neither in Singapore nor in Hongkong nor in Manila did I agree to recognize verbally nor in writing, American domination over our beloved country. I declare that while I was transported to Cavite [a province in the Philippines] on board one of their naval vessels, I immediately made known in a Manifesto addressed to the Filipinos, my determination to wage war against Spain to win our independence. I reiterated this on the day when for the first time, I hoisted our flag, the emblem of our legitimate aspirations….

Natives and foreigners have witnessed that American soldiers have rendered publicly on many occasions, military honors to our flag, recognizing us as belligerents.

As it is stated in the Proclamation of General Otis that in accordance with the instructions of the President of the United States they will be engaged in the internal administration of the archipelago. I protest in the name of God, based upon justice and law, that I have been visibly designated to lead my countrymen in the task for their regeneration against this American intrusion. I also protest in the name of all the people in the Philippines; these people have chosen me to lead their destiny; my duty is therefore to fight until my last breath for her independence.

For the last time, I protest again, because of my former relations with the Americans who conducted me from Hongkong to Cavite not to wage war against the Spaniards for their benefit but for us, against their unexpected claim to dominate us.

And it is for this, my dear countrymen you should understand that in the end, united by indissoluble ties, we will not retrogress from the glorious way which is open to us.

---

1. What evidence does Aguinaldo offer to show that he had expected the United States to support independence for the Philippines?

2. What promise does Aguinaldo make to the Filipino people?

3. How would you describe the tone of this manifesto?

Source 3

Mark Twain's Views on Imperialism, Interview in the New York Herald, *October 4, 1900*

Mark Twain, author of *Tom Sawyer* and *Huckleberry Finn*, was one of the best-loved American writers. When he came home after a nine year stay in London, the war against Aguinaldo's forces in the Philippines had been going on for more than a year. A reporter asked Twain for his views.

You ask me about what is called imperialism. Well, I have formed views about that question. I am at the disadvantage of not knowing whether our people are for or against spreading themselves over the face of the globe. I should be sorry if they are, for I don't think that it is wise or a necessary development. As to China, I quite approve of our Government's action in getting free of that complication. They are withdrawing, I understand, having done what they wanted. That is quite right. We have no more business in China than in any other country that is not ours.

There is the case of the Philippines. I have tried hard, and yet I cannot for the life of me comprehend how we got into that mess. Perhaps we could not have avoided it—perhaps it was inevitable that we should come to be fighting the natives of those islands—but I cannot understand it, and have never been able to get at the bottom of the origin of our antagonism to the natives. I thought we should act as their protector—not try to get them under our heel. We were to relieve them from Spanish tyranny to enable them to set up a government of their own, and we were to stand by and see that it got a fair trial. It was not to be a government according to our ideas, but a government that represented the feeling of the majority of the Filipinos, a government according to Filipino ideas. That would have been a worthy mission for the United States. But now—why, we have got into a mess, a quagmire from which each fresh step renders the difficulty of extrication immensely greater. I'm sure I wish I could see what we were getting out of it, and all it means to us as a nation.

1. What is Twain's overall view of imperialism?

2. Twain calls the U.S. war in the Philippines a "quagmire." What do you think he means?

3. What contrast does Twain see between the American role in the Philippines before the Spanish-American War and after?

Source 4

Two Cartoons About the War in the Philippines: Winsor McKay, 1899, and "Take Your Choice," Judge Magazine, 1900

The cartoon on the left appeared as the U.S. war against Filipino nationalists was just beginning. The cartoon on the right appeared as President McKinley was running for re-election against anti-imperialist William Jennings Bryan.

This cartoon was drawn by Winsor McKay, one of America's most popular cartoonists. The figure disappearing over the hill with a basketful of cash represents Spain.

The two figures shown standing on the Philippines are Bryan and McKinley. The caption reads, *TAKE YOUR CHOICE. Do you want a man who, having raised the stars and stripes on our new possessions, will maintain them with dignity; or a man who will cut down "Old Glory" and make us the laughing-stock of the world?*

1. In the cartoon on the left, what is Winsor McKay saying about U.S. policy in the Philippines?

2. Which candidate does the cartoonist on the right favor? Why?

3. How does each cartoonist use images to support his point?

Lesson 1 America Enters World War I

CLOSE READING

The Causes of World War I

1. **Paraphrase** The text calls Europe a "powder keg" in the years leading up to World War I. Explain the meaning of this phrase and why it was used to describe pre-war Europe.

2. **Compare and Contrast** Compare and contrast how Great Britain and Germany prepared their military forces for war.

The Great War Begins

3. **Identify Supporting Details** What were Germany's motives in invading Belgium and then France in July of 1914?

4. **Identify Cause and Effect** Why did a stalemate develop on the Western Front during World War I? Why were there so many more casualties in World War I than in earlier wars?

The United States Remains Neutral

5. **Categorize** Fill in the graphic organizer below to show the three distinct positions that divided U.S. public opinion about the war in Europe.

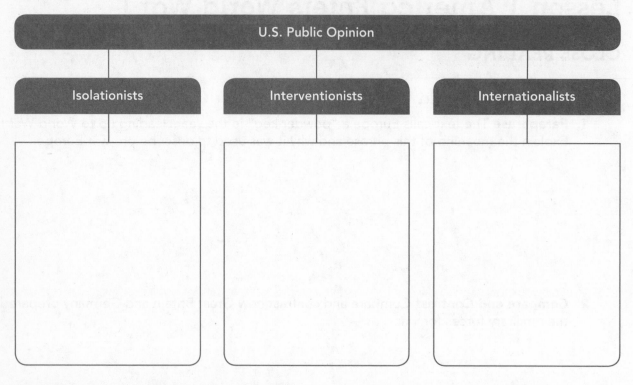

U.S. Public Opinion		
Isolationists	Interventionists	Internationalists

Reasons for U.S. Entry into the War

6. **Draw Inference** Why did the United States find Germany's U-boats more problematic than the British naval blockade?

7. **Explain an Argument** Why did the Germans believe that the bombing of the *Lusitania* was justified? Why were the British outraged by this event?

8. **Draw Conclusions** Why did Americans find the Zimmermann note so threatening?

Lesson 2 The Home Front During World War I

CLOSE READING

Mobilizing for War

1. **Evaluate Explanations** Was it necessary for the U.S. government to get involved in private industry during wartime? Explain why or why not.

Opposition to the War

2. **Draw Conclusions** How were pacifists and conscientious objectors treated during World War I? Why were they treated this way?

3. **Identify Supporting Details** Use the graphic organizer below to identify the positive and negative aspects of the work of the Committee on Public Information (CPI) during World War I. Use information from the previous text as well as this one.

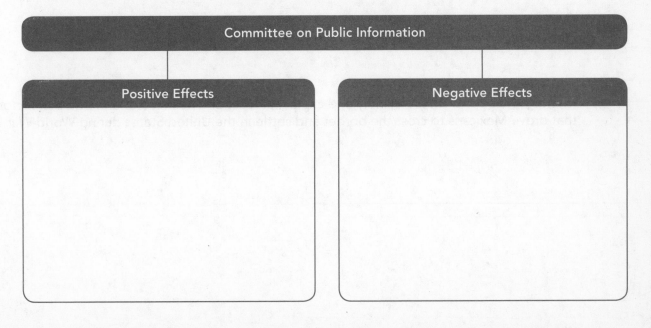

Committee on Public Information

Positive Effects	Negative Effects

4. **Summarize** How did the United States government limit people's freedoms during World War I? Why?

5. **Draw Conclusions** What was the national sentiment toward the Germans during World War I? Support your conclusion using evidence from the text.

The War Changes American Society

6. **Categorize** Describe the "push" and "pull" factors that caused African Americans to move to the North during the Great Migration.

7. **Identify Cause and Effect** Identify and explain at least one push factor and one pull factor that drove Mexicans to cross the border and settle in the United States during World War I.

Lesson 3 The End of World War I

CLOSE READING

America Joins the Fighting

1. **Identify Cause and Effect** How did the Russian Revolution affect the situation on the Western Front?

2. **Draw Inferences** Why did General Pershing want to keep the American Expeditionary Forces independent?

Wilson Wants "Peace Without Victory"

3. **Evaluate Explanations** Lenin claimed that World War I was an "imperialistic land-grab." Do you agree? Why or why not? Use evidence from the text to support your position.

4. **Paraphrase** Explain what Wilson meant by "peace without victory," and why he compared peace with victory to quicksand in his "Peace Without Victory" speech.

The Paris Peace Conference

5. **Draw Conclusions** Why were many countries in Europe opposed to portions of Wilson's Fourteen Points?

America Rejects the Treaty of Versailles

6. **Categorize** Use the graphic organizer below to describe the different factions of senators that formed during the vote for the Treaty of Versailles. Include information about the leaders of each party, their beliefs, and how they viewed Article 10 and America's role in world affairs.

Voting Factions

Irreconcilables	Reservationists	Supporters

7. **Draw Conclusions** Why was Wilson willing to compromise in Versailles, but not in Washington, D.C.?

Lesson 4 The Postwar Economy Booms

CLOSE READING

Postwar Issues

1. **Summarize** Explain how the large numbers of soldiers returning from fighting in World War I affected the lives of women and African Americans.

2. **Identify Cause and Effect** What were some of the negative effects of the inflation that occurred after World War I?

3. **Draw Inferences** Use evidence from the text to make inferences about the amount of power that workers had in the 1920s.

The Impact of Henry Ford and the Automobile

4. **Identify Cause and Effect** Describe at least two ways the Model T stimulated the economy.

5. **Draw Conclusions** The invention of the Model T had several effects on how people lived. In your opinion, what was the most significant social effect of the Model T? Cite evidence to support your conclusion.

Economic Growth in the 1920s

6. **Draw Conclusions** The text mentions that some advertisers focused on the desires and fears of consumers. How does the advertisement for the breakfast cereal do this? Can you name a modern commercial that exploits people's desires or fears in order to sell a product?

7. **Summarize** How did buying on margin and installment buying affect consumer behavior?

Urban, Suburban, and Rural Areas

8. **Compare and Contrast** How did social trends in the 1920s help increase social divisions between rural and urban areas?

Lesson 5 Government in the 1920s

CLOSE READING

The Harding Administration

1. **Analyze Interactions Among People and Events** What political change did President Harding's election represent?

2. **Draw Inferences** What message did Harding send when he appointed Andrew Mellon as Secretary of the Treasury? Did Mellon's actions match Harding's message?

3. **Determine Central Ideas** Use the graphic organizer below to record the central idea and supporting details in the last two sections: "Some Officials Betray the Public Trust" and "The Teapot Dome Scandal Comes to Light."

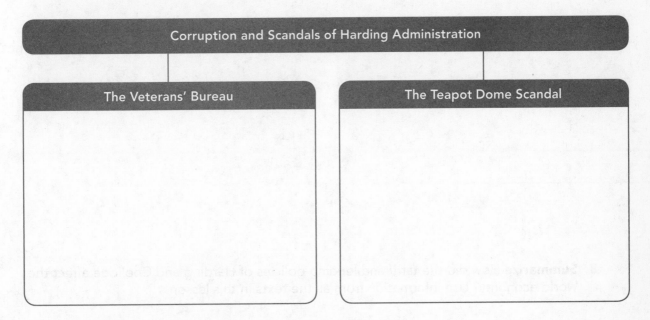

Corruption and Scandals of Harding Administration

The Veterans' Bureau

The Teapot Dome Scandal

Economic Prosperity Under Coolidge

4. **Cite Evidence** What policies of Harding and Coolidge are still being pursued today?

America's Place in a Changed World

5. **Explain an Argument** Why did some Congressmen advise forgiving the war debts?

6. **Draw Inferences** Why do you think that diplomats and politicians worked on the Kellogg-Briand Pact if they believed it was "unenforceable"?

7. **Assess an Argument** Did the Dawes Plan solve the problem of war debt? Why or why not?

8. **Summarize** How did the tariff and lending policies of Harding and Coolidge affect the world economy? Use information from all the texts in this lesson.

Lesson 6 An Unsettled Society

CLOSE READING

Americans Debate New Ideas and Values

1. **Compare and Contrast** Use the graphic organizer below to contrast the values that clashed in the United States during the 1920s.

Rural Areas	Urban Areas

2. **Analyze Interactions Among People and Events** Why did the Scopes Trial become a public spectacle? Analyze information from the text in your answer.

The Red Scare

3. **Analyze Sequence** How did communism in the Soviet Union contribute to the rise and ebbing of the Red Scare in the United States?

Immigration in the 1920s

4. **Identify Cause and Effect** What sentiments in the United States led to the rigid immigrant quotas in the 1920s?

5. **Summarize** What was the intent of the National Origins Act? Was the law fair? Use evidence from the text in your explanation.

The Ku Klux Klan in the Early 1900s

6. **Draw Conclusions** Why was the revived Ku Klux Klan able to spread beyond the South and into some urban areas?

7. **Cite Evidence** Explain how members of the NAACP and Jewish Anti-Defamation League defended American values when faced with the hatred of the Ku Klux Klan. Cite evidence from the text in your answer.

Prohibition Divides Americans

8. **Analyze Interactions Among People and Events** Explain how Prohibition was related to the rise in organized crime during the 1920s.

Lesson 7 The Roaring Twenties

CLOSE READING

Popular American Culture in the 1920s

1. **Summarize** In the Venn diagram below, show how life differed for people in urban and rural areas. In the overlap section, list the new forms of entertainment that were enjoyed by people in both rural and urban areas.

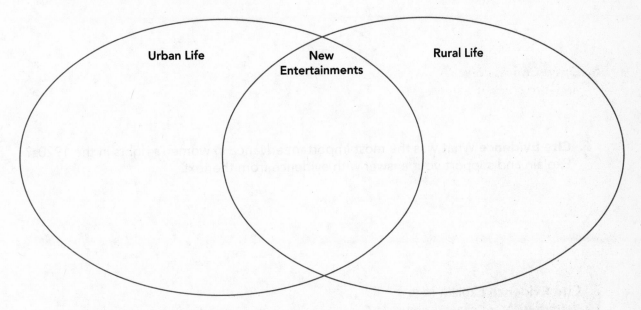

2. **Summarize** Why were silent films so successful during the 1920s? Give at least two reasons.

American Role Models

3. **Draw Conclusions** Americans were obsessed with heroes like Babe Ruth and Charles Lindbergh in the 1920s. Why did both men appeal to Americans at the time?

4. **Identify Supporting Details** Give an example of how technological innovations during the 1920s have become important in modern American life.

The Role of Women Changes

5. Draw Inferences The text argues that flappers in the 1920s were an expression of social change. What kind of change did flappers represent?

6. Cite Evidence What was the most important advance in women's rights in the 1920s? Explain and support your answer with evidence from the text.

Social Issues Are Reflected in Art and Literature

7. Determine Author's Point of View Read the excerpt from *The Great Gatsby* by F. Scott Fitzgerald. What point did Fitzgerald want to make through his descriptions of Gatsby and his parties?

Lesson 8 The Harlem Renaissance

CLOSE READING

Support for Black Nationalism in Urban Areas

1. **Compare and Contrast** How did Marcus Garvey's ideas differ from those of W.E.B. Du Bois or Booker T. Washington?

2. **Identify Supporting Details** In what ways did African Americans continue to experience prejudice as they moved to the North? Give a few examples from the text.

The Jazz Age

3. **Paraphrase** Explain why F. Scott Fitzgerald called the 1920s the "Jazz Age."

4. **Analyze Interactions Among People and Events** What groups, places, and events influenced the creation of jazz music?

5. **Identify Cause and Effect** Give at least two examples of how jazz music influenced popular culture.

The Harlem Renaissance

6. **Draw Conclusions** What tensions and conflicts characterized the Harlem Renaissance? Give at least two examples.

7. **Compare and Contrast** Zora Neale Hurston and Langston Hughes were both important figures in the Harlem Renaissance. Explain how their voices and the ideas they conveyed were similar.

PRIMARY SOURCE EXPLORATION

Homing in on the Harlem Renaissance

Introduction

During the 1920s, African Americans created an artistic movement that influenced and reshaped the culture of modern America and the world. This movement, known today as the Harlem Renaissance, was centered in the Black neighborhood of Harlem in New York City. At a time when African Americans faced discrimination and racist violence, the achievements of the writers, musicians, and artists of the Harlem Renaissance transformed the way African Americans viewed themselves and paved the way for the civil rights movement that eventually followed.

Document-Based Writing Activity

Analyze the following four sources and then use information from the documents and your knowledge of world history to write an essay in which you

- Describe how the Great Migration helped create conditions that led to the Harlem Renaissance.
- Discuss how the Harlem Renaissance created confidence and pride in African American achievement.

Keep in mind that your essay should include an introduction, several paragraphs, and a conclusion. In the body of the essay, use evidence from at least three documents. Support your response with relevant facts, examples, and details. In developing your essay, be sure to keep these general definitions in mind:

- *Describe* means "to illustrate something in words or tell about it."
- *Discuss* means "to make observations about something using facts, reasoning, and argument; to present in some detail."

Source 1

Letter from Rampy J. Burdick to Attorney General John G. Sargeant, March 3, 1928

In the early 1900s, African Americans were still struggling against the forces of racism and discrimination. In many places they faced campaigns of terror waged by the Ku Klux Klan and their sympathizers, as well as the indifference of authorities who did little to protect them or defend their rights as American citizens.

Attorney General Sargeant
National Capitol
Washington, D.C.

Dear Sir:

Eighteen months ago a mob under guise of the K.K.K. attacked and drove my father from (his bed) his dwelling, about midnight. Due to terror a very young brother of mine was forced to flee from the house, from whence he went to a newly plowed field where he buried himself in a deep furrow [trench]. Out of fear for his life, my father, dressed in a very thin night gown, escaped to a nearby copse [group of trees] where he spent most of the night in a drizzle. After the effort of the felons [criminals, here meaning Klan members] to get my father was foiled they battered down a door against which my mother and sister (frantically) pushed to stay them; they riddled another door with bullets. . . .

We, the Burdick family, haven't sufficient money to investigate thoroughly and prosecute, that is bring these curs [dogs, here meaning hateful people] to justice. Through the months that have passed since this occurrence, my father has (through) discussion seen it necessary to go well armed; he has found that he has had to do much that the state should have done, that is guard his life. We, my father and I, are tax payers and citizens of the United States. Since the country and the state have failed to act upon this Constitutional offense, I supplicate [beg] you in the name of peace, liberty, happiness, and life to see that action is had.

My father and his family reside at Ethridge, Tenn. (G.U. Burdick)

Very sincerely yours,

Rampy J. Burdick

1. According to this account, what effect did the K.K.K. attack have on the Burdick family?

2. Why is Burdick appealing to the Attorney General of the United States rather than to local and state authorities for help?

3. Why does Burdick point out that he and his father are tax payers and citizens?

Source 2

"Spring to See Greatest Migration in History," **Chicago Defender, February 20, 1925**

When this article was published, the massive migration of African Americans from the South to the industrial cities of the North had been underway for about fifteen years. By the mid-1920s, the effects of this migration were dramatic and transformative. Throughout the country, African Americans neighborhoods grew in size and prosperity, creating a large, educated Black middle class and launching a cultural awakening.

The great northward trek [long journey] is on again. Memphis, the assembling point for those who have turned their faces northward, is fast becoming crowded with persons from farther south who are patiently awaiting the opportunity to cross the line into a free country [here meaning the North].

All winter, according to reports issued by social agencies, families have been pouring into Memphis and literally "camping." These people are tired of working all summer for nothing, starving in winter, refused proper educational facilities and civic protections, and tired of seeing their homes at the constant mercy of bigoted whites. In this city the travelers have been advised to halt a brief minute until spring has cleared up the atmosphere farther north and the business opportunities have become more promising. . .

Throughout southern Tennessee, Georgia and Mississippi farm huts are being deserted. In certain sections of Mississippi entire plantations, where once white planters thrived by robbing and cheating their laborers, are being deserted. Sections where, at this time last year the plowing was being done, are now lying idle. . . . .

"For years we have lived in Mississippi," declared one father, "and have worked for the same man. I work hard, as do the rest of my family, and yet we stay in debt. The man we worked for on shares [as sharecroppers] always cheated us and we could do nothing about it. My children were forced to go three miles to school and could only go there three months out of the year, while white children attended nine months out of every year. The separate schools is only a scheme to give us inferior education. . . ."

The people have grown tired waiting for what they have already earned. They are moving into that part of the country that at least recognizes them as human beings. And the spring will see one of the most widespread, most concerted, migrations in the history of this country.

1. According to this account, why is the Great Migration underway?

2. In the list of reasons that this article gives for leaving the South, what phrase confirms what you have learned about the treatment of African Americans in Source 1?

3. What effect is the migration having on the South?

Source 3

Harlem, Mecca of the New Negro, Alain Locke, from Survey Graphic, *March 1925*

In the 1920s, African Americans, using the terminology of the time, called it the New Negro movement. Today, we call it the Harlem Renaissance because some of its most exciting developments occurred in the Harlem neighborhood of New York City. One of the leading writers who defined this movement was Alain Locke, an African American philosopher. In this excerpt, he describes the changes reshaping American culture.

In the last decade something beyond the watch and guard of statistics has happened in the life of the American Negro and the three norms who have traditionally presided over the Negro problem have a changeling [a child who has changed identity] in their laps. The Sociologist, The Philanthropist, the Race-leader are not unaware of the New Negro, but they are at a loss to account for him. He simply cannot be swathed in their formulae. For the younger generation is vibrant with a new psychology; the new spirit is awake in the masses, and under the very eyes of the professional observers is transforming what has been a perennial problem into the progressive phases of contemporary Negro life. . . .

. . .the mind of the Negro seems suddenly to have slipped from under the tyranny of social intimidation and to be shaking off the psychology of imitation and implied inferiority. By shedding the old chrysalis of the Negro problem we are achieving something like a spiritual emancipation. Until recently, lacking self-understanding, we have been almost as much of a problem to ourselves as we still are to others. But the decade that found us with a problem has left us with only a task. The multitude perhaps feels as yet only a strange relief and a new vague urge, but the thinking few know that in the reaction the vital inner grip of prejudice has been broken.

With this renewed self respect and self-dependence, the life of the Negro community is bound to enter a new dynamic phase, the buoyancy from within compensating for whatever pressure there may be of conditions from without. The migrant masses, shifting from countryside to city, hurdle several generations of experience at a leap, but more important, the same thing happens spiritually in the life attitudes and self-expression of the Young Negro, in his poetry, his art, his education and his new outlook, with the additional advantage, of course, of the poise and greater certainty of knowing what it is all about.

1. What does Locke mean by "the vital inner grip of prejudice has been broken"?

2. In the third paragraph, what is Locke saying about the Great Migration and the new movement?

3. What is the connection that Locke makes between the arts and this new "spiritual emancipation"?

Source 4

Book Cover by Aaron Douglas of Claude McKay's Novel Home to Harlem, _1928_

The artists, writers, and musicians of the Harlem Renaissance thrived on the cosmopolitan atmosphere of New York City and its international connections. New York had particularly strong cultural links with Paris, where modern art movements were inspiring an interest in abstract forms and a new appreciation of African art. Aaron Douglas' illustration shown here combines Parisian cubist shapes with African stylization.

1. Study the image and the book title. How does the graphic hint at the subject matter of the novel? What details suggest travel?

2. Which aspects of the buildings symbolize Harlem and New York?

3. What emotions does this image convey?

Lesson 1 Causes of the Depression

CLOSE READING

Hidden Economic Problems in the Roaring Twenties

1. **Analyze Interactions Among People and Events** How did many farmers get into debt in the 1920s? Explain how World War I and crop prices affected farmers during this time period.

2. **Identify Supporting Details** What problems did industrial workers face in the 1920s? Give two examples.

3. **Summarize** Explain why the large gap between the rich and the poor led to economic instability.

The Stock Market Hits Bottom

4. **Identify Cause and Effect** What role did credit and speculation play in the stock market crash?

The Great Depression Begins

5. Identify Cause and Effect Use the cause and effect chart below to explain some of the effects of the stock market crash. Include at least three effects in your chart.

Causes	Effects
• The stock market crashed in 1929.	

6. Summarize What was the goal of the Hawley-Smoot Tariff? Was the tariff successful?

7. Analyze Interactions Explain how the depression in the United States affected the economy of Europe.

The Causes of the Great Depression

8. Draw Conclusions What government actions would Keynes have recommended to prevent the depression?

Lesson 2 Americans Suffer

CLOSE READING

Economic Hardship Shakes the Cities

1. Draw Conclusions How might it have affected people's morale to wait in unemployment lines and bread lines to keep their families nourished and alive? Use the photographs and the text to help you draw conclusions.

2. Compare and Contrast How did the depression impact workers who were able to keep their jobs? How was this similar to and different from the impact on workers who lost their jobs?

3. Draw Inferences During the Great Depression, Americans called shantytowns "Hoovervilles," newspapers "Hoover blankets," and their empty pants pockets "Hoover flags." What does this reveal about how they felt about Herbert Hoover?

Rural America Struggles with Poverty

4. Identify Cause and Effect What chain of events caused the dust storms on the Great Plains?

5. **Identify Supporting Details** Give three details or examples that support the following main idea: The Dust Bowl storms were devastating to farmers.

6. **Use Visual Information** Analyze the photograph of the Missouri family packing up to head west in "Rural America Struggles With Poverty." What challenges might a family like this face as they traveled west in search of jobs?

Hard Times Hit Most Americans

7. **Analyze Style and Rhetoric** What is the tone of Clifford Burke's writing in the excerpt from *Hard Times*? What does he believe about African Americans and white people?

8. **Draw Inferences** Who or what did Americans blame for their misfortunes during the Great Depression? Give three examples.

Lesson 3 Two Presidents Respond

CLOSE READING

Hoover's Response Fails

1. **Draw Conclusions** What assumptions did Hoover have about the forces that had caused the depression?

2. **Summarize** Why did Hoover prefer to give money to railroads, banks, and large businesses rather than individuals?

Challenging Economic Times Lead to Protest

3. **Cite Evidence** Did Hoover handle the Bonus Army march well? Use primary and secondary sources to explain why or why not.

Americans Turn to Roosevelt

4. **Compare and Contrast** How was Franklin D. Roosevelt's approach to fighting the depression different than Herbert Hoover's approach?

5. Use Visual Information Study the map showing the results of the 1932 presidential election. What gave Roosevelt such a clear mandate for his policies?

The New Deal Begins

6. Identify Supporting Details Explain the idea behind the Agricultural Adjustment Act (AAA). What were the goals, advantages, and disadvantages of this act?

7. Draw Conclusions FDR's New Deal established many important, far-reaching programs. List and explain two programs that still impact the U.S. government today.

Critics of the New Deal

8. Summarize Explain two criticisms of FDR's New Deal, from different sides of the political spectrum.

Lesson 4 The New Deal Expands

CLOSE READING

Expanding New Deal Programs

1. **Analyze Interactions Among Events** Identify three of the most significant impacts of the second New Deal.

2. **Vocabulary: Determine Meaning** Explain the meaning of *pump priming* in your own words.

3. **Cite Evidence** What was the most significant advantage and the most significant disadvantage of the Social Security program? Cite evidence for your views.

Labor Unions Thrive

4. **Identify Supporting Details** How did FDR's New Deal programs help workers? Give two examples.

5. **Draw Conclusions** Why did sit-down strikes, such as the UAW strike in 1936, improve worker rights? Use evidence from primary and secondary sources.

Opposition to the New Deal

6. **Assess an Argument** Discuss FDR's plan to add more justices to the Supreme Court. Would adding justices to the Supreme Court increase the power of the executive branch? Explain why or why not.

7. **Analyze Interactions Among Events** How did the condition of the economy affect the 1936 election?

8. **Identify Cause and Effect** Why did FDR choose not to focus on additional New Deal programs in the late 1930s? Explain at least two causes.

Lesson 5 Effects of the New Deal

CLOSE READING

Women Play Increasingly Significant Political Roles

1. **Identify Supporting Details** Identify at least three ways Eleanor Roosevelt was able to influence U.S. policy.

A Stronger Political Voice for African Americans

2. **Summarize** What was life like for African Americans during FDR's administration? Support your answer with evidence.

New Deal Legislation for American Indians

3. **Draw Inferences** Why did dividing up tribal lands cause so many Native Americans to lose their lands?

4. **Explain an Argument** What was the goal of the Navajo Livestock Reduction program? What were the issues with it?

A New Political Coalition Emerges

5. Draw Conclusions Why was FDR able to win so many terms as President?

6. Assess an Argument What was the most significant voting bloc gained by FDR?

New Deal Legislation Expands the Historical Role of Government

7. Identify Supporting Details Explain how the federal government became a more significant presence in the lives of ordinary Americans during the New Deal. Give at least three examples.

8. Summarize Explain at least one negative effect of New Deal legislation.

Lesson 6 Culture During the Depression

CLOSE READING

A New Age in American Entertainment

1. Summarize How did movies in the 1930s demonstrate the public's changing view of the government?

2. Identify Supporting Details List three facts that support this main idea: Mass media became widespread and accessible in the 1930s.

3. Draw Conclusions Why did so many people watch movies and listen to the radio during the Great Depression?

Increased Funding for the Arts

4. Draw Inferences Why did the government help support the arts in the 1930s?

5. **Paraphrase** Based on Roy Stryker's quote, what were Dorothea Lange's photos like? Did she achieve the goal of showing city people what it was like to live on a farm?

6. **Determine Central Idea** What is the central idea of the Coit Tower mural shown in "Increased Funding for the Arts"? Point out any other details you notice.

The Depression Era Reflected in Literature

7. **Summarize** What sentiments did African Americans express in the literature, movies, and art of the 1930s?

8. **Draw Conclusions** Identify two major themes in the literature of the 1930s. Include examples in your description.

PRIMARY SOURCE EXPLORATION

The Changing U.S. Attitude Toward Mexican Workers

Introduction

During the dark days of the depression, Mexicans and Mexican Americans who had lived in the United States for years suddenly found they were no longer welcome. The United States began deporting, or repatriating, both Mexican immigrants and American citizens of Mexican ancestry. But just a few years later, beginning in 1942, the United States and Mexico signed a series of agreements creating the bracero program, which allowed Mexican men to work legally as temporary laborers in the United States. Appalling economic conditions, terrible poverty, and high crime rates in Mexico pushed millions of Mexican men to seize the opportunity to help their families by joining the program. Working from sunup to sundown for wages that many American workers would have refused, the men found that the decent housing and food they had been promised didn't always materialize. Still, they labored on, in hopes of better days ahead.

Document-Based Writing Activity

Analyze the following four sources and then use information from the documents and your knowledge of American history to write an essay in which you

- Discuss the changing attitude in the United States toward workers from Mexico.
- Explain the role played by the economy in shaping this attitude toward Mexicans and Mexican Americans in the 1930s and 1940s.

Keep in mind that your essay should include an introduction, several paragraphs, and a conclusion. In the body of the essay, use evidence from at least three documents. Support your response with relevant facts, examples, and details. In developing your essay, be sure to keep these general definitions in mind:

- *Discuss* means "to make observations about something using facts, reasoning, and argument; to present in some detail."
- *Explain* means "to make plain or understandable; to give reasons for or causes of; or to show the logical development or relationships of."

Source 1

Telegram from C. P. Visel to Colonel Arthur M. Woods, January 6, 1931

In 1931, the Los Angeles Citizens Committee wanted to deport the city's Mexican immigrants. In this telegram, C. P. Visel, the committee's coordinator, reaches out to a government official for advice on how to carry out the deportations.

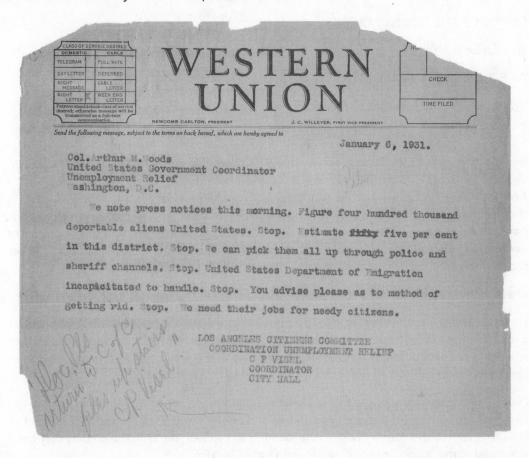

1. What particular section of the Los Angeles Citizens Committee was Visel in charge of?

2. What method does Visel propose for deporting immigrants from Los Angeles?

3. What reason does Visel give for wanting to deport the immigrants who live in Los Angeles?

Source 2

Letter from Pablo Guerrero to the Los Angeles County Clerk, May 28, 1934

In this letter to the Los Angeles County Clerk, Pablo Guerrero asks to be lawfully readmitted into the United States. His request was denied.

OFFICE OF THE COUNTY CLERK

Translation from Spanish to English   A. G. Rivera   Date 6/1/34

INTERPRETERS' DIVISION 31336

V. LYLE DEPUTY CLERK IN CHARGE

5/28/34. Mexicali, Low. Calif. Mexico. L.A. County. Los Angeles, Cfa.

By these presents [documents] I hereby make it known that my family and myself were deported into Mexico on 12/8/32, on the S.P. [Southern Pacific] trains that left Los Angeles, Calif., and in view of the fact that all of my children were born in the U.S. of A, they do not like the Mexican customs and wish to return to the U.S. in company with their parents and ask the Los Angeles County authorities, as a favor to address the Department of Labor in Washington, requesting that the American Consulate in Mexicali, Low. Cfa. be ordered to grant me immigration papers, paying $18.00 for each Passport.

I have worked all of my life, since I was 19 years of age in the U.S. of A.

I want to arrange everything legally; I do not wish to violate the frontier Immigration Law, and I want my Passport issued with the seal of an American citizen. I worked in the U.S. of A. since 1904 with different companies. I registered in the world war in Johnson, Arizona, Cochise Co.

I have never given my services to the Mexican government nor to the Mexican capital. I have worked all of my life, since I was 19 years of age in the U.S. of A., and that is why I wish to return to the country where I am entitled to live with my children so that they be educated in the schools of your country and not in Mexico.

Besides, the Mexican Government does not give any assistance nor protection to children born in the U.S. of A., and for that reason I ask that my children and myself be allowed to return to the country in which they are entitled to live. . . .

---

1. Why are Guerrero and his family living in Mexico?

2. What arguments does Guerrero make to convince officials to readmit him and his family to the United States?

3. Guerrero's oldest child was born in 1918 and his youngest in 1926. How does this fact pertain to his argument that his children should be readmitted to the United States?

Source 3

"Americans All" Poster by Leon Helguera, January 1943

As World War II raged on, the United States tried to repair its relationship with Mexicans and Mexican Americans because their labor was desperately needed on the home front. In late 1942, an official at the Office of War Information (OWI) issued a memo noting several themes for new OWI posters. Among them, a plea for the help of Mexican Americans "in the American armed forces, in American factories, and on American farms."

AMERICANOS TODOS
★
LUCHAMOS POR LA VICTORIA

★ **AMERICANS ALL** ★
LET'S FIGHT FOR VICTORY

1. What symbolism does this poster use to inspire Mexicans and Mexican Americans to join the war effort?

2. How is the wording on this poster a call for unity among neighboring nations?

3. How might winning the support of Mexican Americans have furthered the goal of obtaining labor from Mexico?

Source 4

Interview with Bracero Worker Agustín Martínez Olivares, 2003

Posters and propaganda didn't bring in enough labor to keep American farms going during World War II. In 1942, one governor, Culbert Olson of California, sent a telegram to the secretaries of state, labor, and agriculture noting that "Without a substantial number of Mexicans the situation is certain to be disastrous. . . ."

Laureano Martinez (LM): What did you hear about braceros and what they were going to do?

Agustín Martínez Olivares (AM): The first time, back in the ranch people would say many things. That we were going to be sent to war and so many things. I would say 'Don't believe that, and so what if we go to war. With God's help we will come back or maybe not. But we are going to work and make some money.' My wife, God bless her soul, and the other women were nervous thinking that we were going to war. When she wrote in a letter 'Are you in a war?' I said 'Yes, in a war, but of picking cotton.' (Laughs)

LM: What made you decide to go to the United States?

AM: Well, things were difficult and many were going and coming back with some money. I thought that I could give it a try and I got in. Then I was going every year. . . . From Monterrey we took the train, the freight and passengers train. We were all in there. It was filled with many people.

LM: How many people?

AM: Well, all the wagons were full, every car of the train, with passengers already inside and more boarding there. . . .

LM: At what time did you start to work?

AM: Very early. As soon as we could see ourselves. Then we would come back to eat around one or two in the afternoon. And back to work until we could barely see each other.

LM: From sunrise to sunset.

AM: Well, that's what we were there for. Yep, from sunrise to sunset. . . .

1. What rumor was circulating in Mexico about what braceros would do in the U.S.?

2. What can you glean from this interview about the popularity of the bracero program?

3. What was Mr. Martínez's reason for joining the bracero program? How do you know?

Lesson 1 Rise of Aggressive Dictators

CLOSE READING

Peace Dissolves

1. **Identify Cause and Effect** Why didn't the Treaty of Versailles and the League of Nations create a "lasting peace"?

Strict Regimes in the Soviet Union and Italy

2. **Use Visual Information** How did the combination of fear and propaganda help Stalin maintain power? Use the image of Stalin in the text to support your answer.

3. **Draw Conclusions** Why did many people support Mussolini's pledge of order and efficiency?

Germany and Japan Change Leadership

4. **Compare and Contrast** How were the conditions and sentiments in Germany similar to those in Italy in the 1920s?

5. **Analyze Interactions** How did the economic problems of the 1930s affect foreign policy? Cite evidence from your reading, including actions by Germany, Japan, and other countries in Europe.

Dictators Move to Gain Territory

6. **Cite Evidence** Analyze the "Aggression and Appeasement" chart, which describes how the Allies responded to threats from Germany, Japan, and Italy. How does this chart support Yeats's quote: "The best lack all conviction and the worst are full of passionate intensity"?

7. **Analyze Interactions** How did the Spanish Civil War foreshadow the more aggressive conflicts in World War II?

Aggression Meets Appeasement

8. **Draw Inferences** What effect did the signing of the Munich Pact have on Eastern Europeans?

Lesson 2 America Debates Involvement

CLOSE READING

Roosevelt Criticizes Acts of War

1. **Determine Author's Point of View** Read the paragraph from President Roosevelt's Quarantine speech. Explain his metaphor of creating a quarantine. Does Roosevelt think this quarantine will protect the United States?

War Breaks Out in Europe

2. **Cite Evidence** What evidence supports the idea that the German blitzkrieg was successful?

3. **Integrate Information from Diverse Sources** How did the people of Britain keep up their morale during the events at the beginning of World War II? Use diverse sources, including quotes and photographs, to explain.

American Reaction Is Divided

4. **Categorize** As you read "American Reaction Is Divided," use the graphic organizer below to identify the arguments in the debate between the isolationists and the interventionists.

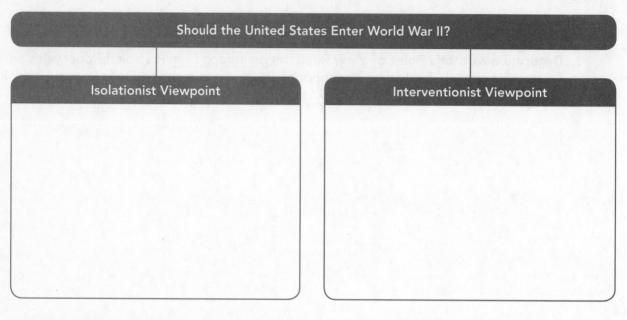

Should the United States Enter World War II?

Isolationist Viewpoint	Interventionist Viewpoint

America Moves Closer Toward War

5. **Draw Inferences** Why did the United States and Britain agree that their priority was defeating Germany, then Japan?

6. **Draw Conclusions** How did the Lend-Lease Act and the Atlantic Charter move the United States away from neutrality?

Lesson 3 The United States Enters World War II

CLOSE READING

Japan Attacks the United States

1. **Identify Cause and Effect** As you read "Japan Attacks the United States," use this graphic organizer to record the causes and effects of the attack on Pearl Harbor.

2. **Integrate Information From Diverse Sources** Read Corpsman Anderson's description of the attack. Then look at the image of the USS *Arizona*. What do Anderson's words and the image convey about the attack? Use specific evidence to support your answer.

3. **Cite Evidence** Roosevelt's "Message Asking for War Against Japan" was broadcast over the radio at the same time he addressed Congress. What do you think was the purpose of this speech? What words in the speech support your answer?

Patriotism Inspires Rapid Mobilization

4. **Identify Supporting Details** Stalin made a toast: "To American production, without which the war would have been lost." What details from the text and its accompanying photos support this main idea?

5. **Use Visual Information** Look at the image of the Liberty Ship *Robert E. Peary* in "Patriotism Inspires Rapid Mobilization." Why was the Liberty Ship considered a production miracle?

6. **Summarize** Explain the roles of African Americans and women in the military in World War II. What prejudice did these groups face?

The Early War in the Pacific

7. **Compare and Contrast** Consider the positions and situations of Japan and the United States in the War in the Pacific in the middle of 1942. Explain the advantages each side had.

212 **Close Reading** ▪ World War II

Lesson 4 A War on Two Fronts

CLOSE READING

Allied Strategy

1. **Compare and Contrast** Describe the goals of Allied and Axis Powers. How were these goals similar and different?

The European Front

2. **Integrate Information From Diverse Sources** Why was the Battle of Stalingrad regarded as "the true turning point of the war in Europe"?

3. **Draw Inferences** How did access to oil fields play an important role in the beginning of World War II?

Axis Powers on the Defensive

4. **Compare and Contrast** the war in Italy to the war in North Africa. Be sure to consider geography, battles, and transportation when you think about the two campaigns.

5. Draw Conclusions Why did Stalin want the Allies to open up another front in France? Why did the Allies avoid doing this until 1944?

6. Summarize What were the goals of Allied bombing runs over Germany? How did saturation and strategic bombing help fulfill these goals?

Turning Points in the Pacific

7. Draw Inferences What impact would a Japanese victory at Midway have on the war in the Pacific? Use the map as well as the text to draw conclusions.

8. Integrate Information From Diverse Sources Examine the photograph of an American soldier on Guadalcanal and read Robert Leckie's description of the island. How might these conditions affect the course of the war in the Pacific?

Lesson 5 The Home Front

CLOSE READING

Patriotism on the Home Front

1. **Identify Supporting Details** How did Americans on the home front contribute to the war effort? Fill in the bubbles on the graphic organizer below as you give examples.

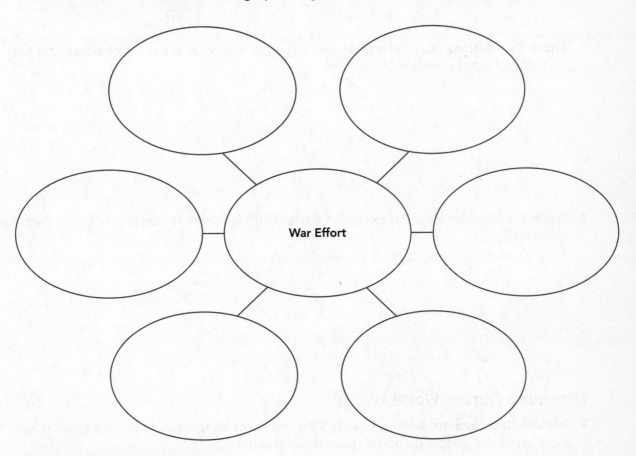

War Effort

Japanese Incarceration

2. **Explain an Argument** Why were Japanese Americans placed in incarceration camps, while Italian Americans and German Americans were not?

3. **Determine Author's Point of View** What were the effects of incarceration on Japanese Americans? Refer to Ted Nakashima's quote in your response.

Increased Opportunities in Employment

4. **Summarize** Many American women had worked outside the home before World War II. What was different about the women working during the war?

5. **Draw Conclusions** How did images like Rosie the Riveter and the act of working in the factories affect the morale of women?

6. **Draw Conclusions** How did Executive Order 8802 fall short in meeting A. Philip Randolph's demands?

Migration During World War II

7. **Identify Interactions Among Events** Why did farms experience labor shortages during the war? What did people do about these labor shortages?

8. **Identify Cause and Effect** How were the causes of the Detroit race riots and the Los Angeles zoot suit riots similar?

Lesson 6 The Allies Win the War

CLOSE READING

Planning Germany's Defeat

1. **Determine Central Ideas** What is the central idea of the joint statement from the Big Three at the Teheran Conference?

The Invasion of Normandy

2. **Identify Supporting Details** What did the Allies do to improve the chance that the D-Day invasion would be successful? Give specific examples.

3. **Determine Central Ideas** How did D-Day help with the liberation of Paris?

Defeat of Germany

4. **Identify Cause and Effect** How did the D-Day invasion and then the Allied invasion of France affect Germany's strategy during World War II?

5. Summarize What was the military significance of the Battle of the Bulge?

Americans Advance Toward Japan

6. Draw Inferences Why did the fighting in the Pacific result in so many casualties for the United States?

7. Use Visual Information Study and analyze the image of destruction in Tokyo. How might this kind of bombing have affected the Japanese?

The War Comes to an End

8. Integrate Information From Diverse Sources Describe the power of the atomic bomb. Use Isao Kita's quote and the photograph of the explosion to support your answer.

Lesson 7 The Holocaust

CLOSE READING

Roots of the Holocaust

1. **Identify Key Steps in a Process** What was Hitler's first step in his anti-Semitic campaign? How did this step pave the way for later developments?

2. **Summarize** Why did the United States refuse to accept the refugees on the *St. Louis*? What were the consequences of this decision?

Hitler's "Final Solution"

3. **Summarize** How did Nazi Germany's persecution of the Jews progress during the war?

4. **List** What groups in addition to Jewish people did the Nazis imprison and murder during the Holocaust?

Allied Response to the Holocaust

5. Summarize Use the graphic organizer to record how the United States reacted to the persecution of European Jews before, during, and after the war.

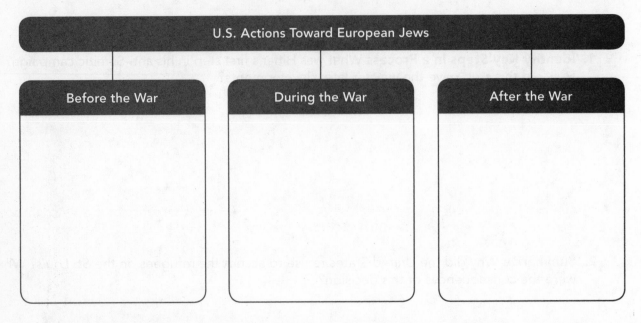

U.S. Actions Toward European Jews

Before the War	During the War	After the War

6. Draw Conclusions Why did it take such a long time for the United States to respond to reports of death camps?

7. Integrate Information From Diverse Sources Review the photographs from the Interactive Gallery: "Inside a Nazi Concentration Camp" and reread the words of U.S. Major Richard Winters. How do the photographs help explain what Winters meant when he said, "Now I know why I'm here"?

Lesson 8 Impact of World War II

CLOSE READING

Planning the Postwar World

1. **Compare and Contrast** the goals of the Yalta Conference and the Potsdam Conference.

2. **Analyze Interactions Among Events** How did the problems that arose at the Potsdam and Yalta conferences foreshadow Cold War conflicts between the United States and the Soviet Union?

International Impact of the War

3. **Compare and Contrast** Why did the Soviet Union and the United States become superpowers after World War II? Explain what made each country strong.

International Organizations and Treaties

4. **Vocabulary: Determine Meaning** The goal of GATT was to expand world trade by reducing tariffs. What is a tariff? Why would reducing tariffs lead to an increase in trade?

5. Explain an Argument After World War II, why did most Americans favor U.S. participation in world organizations such as the United Nations?

6. Paraphrase Reread the excerpt from the Universal Declaration of Human Rights. Restate the meaning of the first sentence in your own words.

Domestic Impact of the War

7. Summarize As you read the text under "Domestic Impact of the War," use the graphic organizer below to list ways that World War II affected the United States both at home and in its relationship with the world.

Effects of World War II

Domestic	International

PRIMARY SOURCE EXPLORATION

On the Front Lines in World War II

Introduction

Midway, Coral Sea, Iwo Jima, D-Day . . . the soldiers who fought in these and other historic battles of World War II are heroes who stood between us and a ruthless enemy who seemed to have little regard for human life. One way we can honor their sacrifices is to try to understand what it was like to serve on the front lines during the war. And one way we can do that is to read first-hand accounts from the soldiers themselves and to look at images taken during this epic struggle between two dramatically different worldviews. When we do, we soon realize that wars are not all about battles. A soldier's experience includes many different aspects of war.

Document-Based Writing Activity

Analyze the following four sources and then use information from the documents and your knowledge of American history to write an essay in which you

- Identify the different experiences described or shown in the sources.
- Evaluate how these experiences might have affected the nation in the years following the war.

Keep in mind that your essay should include an introduction, several paragraphs, and a conclusion. In the body of the essay, use evidence from at least three documents. Support your response with relevant facts, examples, and details. In developing your essay, be sure to keep these general definitions in mind:

- *Identify* means "to find out the defining elements of something."
- *Evaluate* means "to examine and judge the significance, worth, or condition of; to determine the value of."

Source 1

Letter from Guy Vecera, Hawaii, December 1941

Guy Louis Vecera was an American sailor aboard the USS *West Virginia* when it was attacked by the Japanese at Pearl Harbor in 1941. In this excerpt, he describes his experience on that fateful day.

I had the watch on the quarter-deck and was standing by the run-up "colors" when I sighted three bomb hits at the fork of the channel to Pearl Harbor. I ran forward and reported the fact to the Officer of the Day, Ensign Brooks, and as we both looked in that direction we saw a Japanese plane going across our bow with the emblem of the Rising Sun emblazoned boldly on her wings.

Immediately I ran to the deck officer and passed the word "all hands to general quarters" and "close all watertight doors." By this time a torpedo or two had already hit the ship. . . .

By this time the ship was resting on the bottom, but the main deck was still above water. However, the entire forward part of the ship was in flames and the oil on the water around the ship was burning fiercely. Then and only then came the order to "abandon the ship." Men dove over the side and swam to shore about 50 yards distant. . . . I finally reached the starboard side of the "Tennessee" and grabbed hold of her paravane chains to rest for a few minutes. By that time the oil fire on the water had spread so that I could not see the beach. That left me either to be burned by the oil, or drowned, or to attempt climbing up the chains over the bow of the "Tennessee." . . .

I was so tired and weak I didn't believe it possible, but the strength a man has when fighting for his very life, hand over hand, inch by inch, foot by foot, forced me ahead. I crawled painfully up about 30 feet of chain where helping hands helped me down below. By this time the Japs had been beaten off, and I was so completely exhausted I didn't care what happened to me then. . . .

I don't know how I'm going to mail this, as our letters are supposed to be only two pages long, but I'll manage. Give my love to everyone back home and Merry Christmas. . . .

GUY

---

1. How did Vecera know it was the Japanese who were attacking Pearl Harbor?

2. What were the specific threats to Vecera's life?

3. How might Vecera's experience have affected his outlook as an American following the war?

Source 2

Letter from Minoru Masuda, Italy, June 1944

Italy and the Allies signed an armistice in September 1943, at which time the Germans still occupied northern and central Italy. It took nine months, but the Allies finally liberated Rome in June 1944. Minoru Masuda served with the 442nd Regimental Combat Team, a unit made up exclusively of Japanese Americans. He was present in Rome after its liberation.

22 June, 1944

One reason I didn't write sooner was that I had a chance to visit Rome and I was off in a flash. . . . The people here are starving and they have the money. They swarm all over the GIs asking for chocolate, rations, cigarettes etc., especially the first two. A five cent hershey bar will sell for fifty cents, as will a pack of cigarettes.

As for rations, both C and K, they'll part with $1.50. These aren't beggars either—many very well dressed people ask to buy food. The mothers are smart and bring their cute little bambinos and that works tremendously to their advantage, for most GIs are rather tenderhearted in that direction. I had six mashed and battered bars of candy that they grabbed from me for $1.80. You have to fight them off. It's rather pathetic. . . .

Rome as you know is on the Tiber and its history is voluminous. . . . Of course the climax is the St. Peters Cathedral, the home of Catholics, and the Vatican City where the Pope is head man. . . . There are quite a few students from Japan studying here and I happened on one and we chatted both in English and Japanese. He'd been here 9 years and his name was Asahi. He invited us over to his place and we went over after we were through, but he was out. However we met a few of the others and it was strange that we American Japanese should be conversing to a Japan Japanese in Japanese in Italy.

I should be seeing you again soon darling. Keep thinking of me.

1. What experience does Masuda have with the Italian people while in Rome?

2. Why were there Japanese civilians in Rome? How might Masuda's experience with them have altered any preconceived ideas he might have had?

3. How might Masuda's experiences have influenced his outlook related to life after the war, the United States, and racial relations?

Source 3

Letter from Harold Moss, Saipan, July 15, 1944

Harold Moss participated in the successful American attack on the Japanese-held island of Saipan in the Pacific Ocean in 1944. He wrote this letter home shortly after the battle, which was a turning point in the defeat of Japan.

Dear folks:

I should have much to write about this time for the censorship regulations have [been] cut down and now I can tell you some of the many things I have wanted to. As you guessed I am in Saipan on the [Marianas] Islands, about 3200 miles from Hawaii. . . .

. . . [T]he first thing for the night was dig a foxhole and that first one I built was a stinker. I thought it was all right but when our artillery began to fire the thing almost caved in and the sand was all over me. I couldn't hardly get out of the thing for fear of being shot and I wasn't feeling too brave anyway. . . .

Our jeeps have a radio that can get Frisco [San Francisco] and at six o'clock we would listen to the news especially anxious to hear what they had to say about Saipan and hoping you were listening too. But when it came time for the GI programs, an air raid would sound and we would hit for the foxhole. Radio Tokyo is easy to get also and of course we always heard their version too. The reports would be exactly opposite and their reports of casualties about four times what we thought they should be. Tokyo also has a night program called the Zero Hour and dedicated to the American soldiers in the south Pacific. The nerve of the guys. Tokyo Rose speaks perfect English and tries your patience by recalling for you how nice it would be to be home and that sort of stuff. But the music is pretty fair and we don't mind listening. . . .

Love,

Harold

1. Why do you think Tokyo had a radio program for American soldiers?

2. What does this source reveal about life for soldiers outside of battle?

3. How might Moss's experiences have affected his outlook following the war?

Source 4

American and Soviet Troops Meet in Germany, 1945

By early 1945, the Allies had already liberated France and Rome. They continued to move toward Germany from the west, while the Soviets closed in from the east. The armies met outside of Berlin in April, positioning the Allies to attack Hitler's stronghold in Berlin. In the end, however, there was no need. Hitler committed suicide and Germany surrendered less than a month after the photograph at right was taken.

In April 1945, American (left) and Soviet soldiers met at the Elbe River in Torgau, Germany, 50 miles west of Berlin.

1. Describe the expressions on the faces of these soldiers.

2. How is this event similar to one described in Source 2?

3. How might this sort of event have influenced public opinion regarding the Soviet Union in the years after World War II?

Lesson 1 The Beginning of the Cold War

CLOSE READING

Background of the Cold War

1. **Compare and Contrast** the United States and the Soviet Union in the late 1940s. As you read "Background of the Cold War," use the graphic organizer below to take notes about each country's form of government; political ideology, or beliefs, about citizens' rights; and philosophy towards the governance of Germany and Eastern Europe.

	United States	Soviet Union
Forms of Government		
Political Ideology/Beliefs		
Philosophy Toward Governance of Germany/ Eastern Europe		

2. **Use Visual Information** What does the photograph of the Soviet soldier in Berlin reveal about the post-war world?

Responding to the Soviet Challenge

3. **Analyze Style and Rhetoric** What was the main purpose of the Address Before a Joint Session of Congress that President Truman delivered on March 12, 1947? How does Truman's word choice help support that purpose? Give specific examples from the address.

4. Summarize the Truman Doctrine in a sentence or two.

The United States Contains Soviet Expansion

5. Analyze Interactions Among Events What benefits did the Marshall Plan bring to the United States?

6. Draw Conclusions Why did Stalin refuse U.S. aid to the Eastern European countries? What message did his refusal send?

Soviet Aggression Drives the Cold War

7. Cite Evidence Compare the first few "fronts" of the Cold War. Which action was more significant, the Berlin airlift or U.S. aid to Greece and Turkey? Support your answer with evidence from the text.

8. Identify Cause and Effect What events led to the formation of NATO and the Warsaw Pact? What was the purpose of these groups?

Lesson 2 The Korean War

CLOSE READING

China Turns Communist

1. **Determine Central Ideas** As you read "China Turns Communist" and "U.S. Involvement in Korea," use the problem-solution graphic organizer below to note problems and the steps that President Truman took to solve them.

Problem	Solution
• Communists threaten takeover of China.	•

2. **Identify Cause and Effect** What factors led to Mao Zedong's victory in China? Use evidence from the text to trace causes and effects.

U.S. Involvement in Korea

3. **Identify Supporting Ideas** How did U.S. involvement in the conflict between North and South Korea illustrate the Truman Doctrine?

4. Draw Conclusions How did the Korean War involve the United Nations in the Cold War?

5. Compare and Contrast President Truman's and General MacArthur's positions on war with China. Consider not only what each man thought but also how each man's previous experiences influenced his position.

Outcomes of the Korean War

6. Determine Central Ideas What did the United States learn from the Chinese Civil War and the Korean War? Identify a central idea across all of the readings in this lesson.

7. Draw Conclusions How did World War II and the use of the atomic bomb influence U.S. foreign policy in Asia during the 1940s and 1950s?

Lesson 3 The Cold War Intensifies

CLOSE READING

The Arms Race Intensifies Tensions

1. **Identify Cause and Effect** As you read the texts in this lesson, use the chart below to take notes about the relationship between the United States and the Soviet Union. In the first column, note causes, or reasons for the continuing Cold War and arms race. In the second column, note effects, or outcomes of each cause.

Cause		Effect
• The U.S. finds evidence that the Soviet Union has set off an atomic bomb.	The Cold War and arms race	• The U.S. begins to develop and test a hydrogen bomb.

2. **Explain an Argument** Briefly explain the argument that a program of mutually assured destruction prevents countries from actually using weapons of mass destruction against each other. Do you think this argument is valid? Explain why or why not.

Eisenhower's Response to Soviet Aggression

3. **Compare and Contrast** Truman's and Eisenhower's responses to Soviet aggression. How were they similar? How were they different?

4. Categorize What were some benefits of Eisenhower's military policy? What were some drawbacks?

International Cold War Conflicts

5. Analyze Interactions Among People and Events How did events during the Cold War shape future developments in the Middle East? Give at least two examples.

6. Draw Conclusions Did the United States overestimate or underestimate the Soviet Union in the early 1950s? Use evidence from the texts throughout this lesson to support your conclusions.

Lesson 4 Cold War Fears at Home

CLOSE READING

Cold War Tensions Rise at Home

1. **Draw Inferences** What do you think was the most significant impact of the Hollywood Ten and the blacklist and why?

2. **Identify Supporting Details** for the central idea that "no one was above suspicion" of communist activities.

Domestic Spy Cases Increase Fears

3. **Compare and Contrast** As you read "Domestic Spy Cases Increase Fears," use the Venn diagram below to note similarities and differences between the espionage cases of Alger Hiss and the Rosenbergs. Consider both the facts and the impact of the two spy cases.

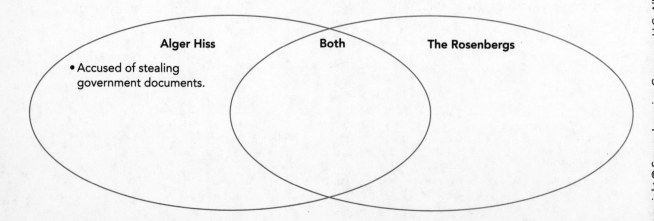

Alger Hiss

• Accused of stealing government documents.

Both

The Rosenbergs

4. Draw Conclusions Why did the Rosenberg case attract so much controversy?

McCarthyism

5. Analyze Interactions Among People and Events Describe the tactics, sentiments, and events that contributed to Senator Joseph McCarthy's success.

6. Draw Inferences What did the downfall of Senator Joseph McCarthy demonstrate about the power of the media?

7. Determine Central Ideas What central idea about McCarthyism is conveyed throughout this lesson?

Lesson 5 Postwar Prosperity

CLOSE READING

Causes and Effects of Prosperity in the 1950s

1. **Recognize Problems and Solutions** As you read "Causes and Effects of Prosperity in the 1950s," use the Problem-Solution graphic organizer below to take notes. In column 1, list problems raised by the shift to a peacetime economy. In column 2, list solutions to the problems.

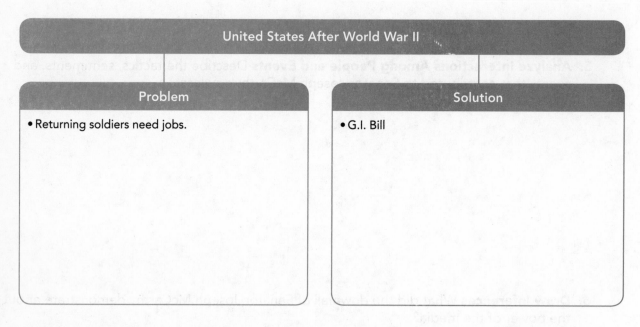

United States After World War II

Problem	Solution
• Returning soldiers need jobs.	• G.I. Bill

2. **Draw Conclusions** How did United States' foreign policy during the late 1940s and early 1950s affect the U.S. economy?

Americans Migrate to the Sunbelt

3. **Analyze Interactions Among Events** Why did so many Americans move to the Sunbelt during the 1950s? What events triggered this trend? What were some of the effects of this trend?

Innovations and Economic Development

4. Summarize how the U.S. workforce changed in the 1950s.

5. Identify Supporting Details Many innovations during the 1950s improved the quality of life for people in the United States. Choose one innovation that you think is especially important and explain its impact.

Truman's Postwar Leadership

6. Compare and Contrast Roosevelt's New Deal and Truman's Fair Deal. Which was more successful? Why?

Eisenhower Leads a Thriving Nation

7. Analyze Interactions Among People and Events The successes of the 1950s were often attributed to Eisenhower. What other factors contributed to America's prosperity during this time period?

Lesson 6 Mass Culture in the 1950s

CLOSE READING

Suburban Migration

1. **Categorize** What "push" and "pull" factors led people to move to the suburbs in the 1950s? As you read "Suburban Migration," take notes on the graphic organizer below. Under "Push" Factors, list factors that pushed Americans out of the city and into the suburbs. Under "Pull" Factors, list factors that attracted Americans to the suburbs.

"Push" Factors	"Pull" Factors

2. **Draw Inferences** How did the rise of the automobile contribute to growth of the suburbs?

Increased Consumption and Consumerism

3. **Summarize** effects of the median family income rising during the 1950s.

Families and Communities in the Fifties

4. Compare and Contrast How did women's "ideal" role change during the 1950s? Contrast this with women's roles in earlier parts of the century.

Educational Opportunities and Priorities

5. Analyze Interactions Among Events Describe events that led to the increase in educational opportunities in the 1950s.

Television Shapes American Culture

6. Determine Author's Point of View David Halberstam is quoted as saying of 1950s family TV shows that "No family problem was so great that it could not be cleared up within the allotted twenty-two minutes." What criticism of these shows does Halberstam make in this statement?

7. Draw Conclusions How did television contribute to the creation of a national mass culture during the 1950s?

Lesson 7 Social Issues of the 1950s

CLOSE READING

Critics and Rebels Emerge

1. **Identify Supporting Details** During the 1950s, different social issues emerged. As you read the lesson, use the graphic organizer below to note social issues that caused discontent among some Americans in the United States.

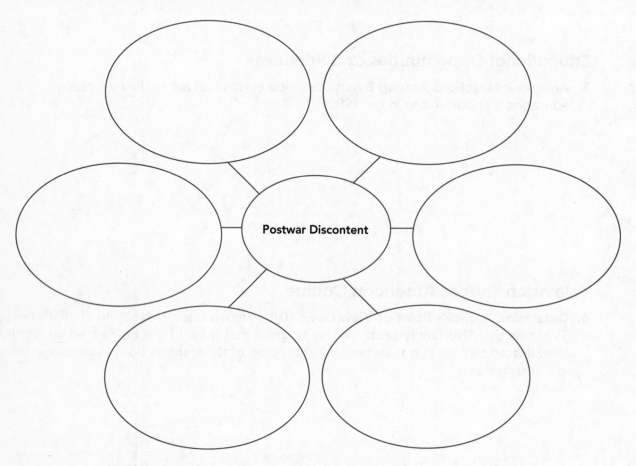

Postwar Discontent

2. **Analyze Interactions** Describe the roots of rock-n-roll music. What other types of music contributed to this style, and how did rock-n-roll music evolve?

Poverty in the Cities and Rural Areas

3. **Analyze Interactions** Explain how the migration of African Americans into urban areas and middle-class whites out of the cities and into the suburbs affected U.S. cities.

4. **Draw Conclusions** Why did urban renewal projects often fail to revitalize urban areas? Use evidence from the text in your answer.

5. **Compare and Contrast** the characteristics of urban and rural poverty in the 1950s. In what ways were they similar? In what ways were they different?

Struggles of Minorities

6. **Draw Inferences** What attracted Mexican immigrants to the bracero program? Why did many continue to participate in this program, despite the difficult conditions?

7. **Summarize** How did some people justify the idea of the termination policy for Native Americans? What were the drawbacks of this policy?

PRIMARY SOURCE EXPLORATION

The Impact of the Berlin Airlift on the Cold War

Introduction

The separation of Germany into four zones occurred after World War II. At first, each superpower controlled a zone. When separation agreements broke down, the Western zone was occupied by the French, British, and the United States. The Eastern zone was occupied by the Soviet Union. In 1948, further disagreements caused the Soviet Union to impose the Berlin Blockade. Access between West Berlin and West Germany was blocked. Nearly two and a half million Berliners lacked access to food and vital supplies. The solution was the Berlin Airlift. But no one was sure it would succeed.

Document-Based Writing Activity

Analyze the following four sources and then use information from the documents and your knowledge of world history to write an essay in which you

- Describe how the Berlin Airlift affected citizens on the home front and citizens in West Berlin.
- Discuss the impact of the Berlin Airlift on the Cold War.

Keep in mind that your essay should include an introduction, several paragraphs, and a conclusion. In the body of the essay, use evidence from at least three documents. Support your response with relevant facts, examples, and details. In developing your essay, be sure to keep these general definitions in mind:

- *Describe* means "to illustrate something in words or tell about it."
- *Discuss* means "to make observations about something using facts, reasoning, and argument; to present in some detail."

Source 1

Summaries of telegraphs to the United States government regarding the Berlin crisis, 1948

During the Berlin Blockade, Western allies (including Austria) supported one another in their opposition of the Soviet government. Below are some telegraphs sent to the United States.

June 28, 1948

Germany We have agreed to a proposal by British Foreign Minister Bevin to maintain a full and complete exchange of information concerning the situation in Germany through our Embassy in London, and we have indicated that for our part we are prepared to continue to maintain our present unprovocative but firm stand in Berlin, utilizing to the utmost the propaganda advantage of our position. Further consideration will be given today to the advisability of sending a three-power note of protest to the Soviet Government.

Ambassador Murphy has pointed out that the presence in Berlin of the western powers has become a symbol of our resistance to Soviet expansionism. It is an index of our prestige in central and eastern Europe and, so far as the Germans are concerned, US presence in Berlin is a measure of US ability and strength in Europe.

Bevin has also expressed the view that western withdrawal from Britain would have serious, if not disastrous, consequences in western German and throughout western Europe. . . .

France A high official of the French Government has informed Embassy Paris that the current instruction to the French Communists are to concentrate all attacks on the US in connection with the German situation, the "Marshall Plan" and especially the bilateral US-French agreement on ECA (Economic Cooperation Administration) assistance.

Austria We have informed our representative in Vienna that we believe there can be no break in the consistent policy of opposing all encroachments by the Soviets on Austrian sovereignty and no indication given that Austria does not enjoy full support of the western powers in maintaining its national independence.

---

1. How will the German government handle the Soviet presence in Western Germany?

2. According to French sources, who would be planning attacks on the U.S.? Who would have directed these attacks?

3. How are the allied nations showing they agree with Truman's containment policy?

Source 2

Impression of a Berlin Airlift Pilot, March 18, 2008

Gail Seymour Halvorsen, a pilot for the allies during the Berlin airlift, gained fame as the Candy Bomber or "Uncle Wiggly Wings" when he started dropping sweets to children in West Berlin. Long after the end of the airlift in 1949, Halvorsen continued to not only attend anniversary celebrations of the airlift in Germany but to further mark the event with candy drops.

Those of us who stayed in the military after the war already knew that the enemy and threat to the West was now Stalin and his Soviet Union. . . . When word came that Stalin had cut off all the food and energy supplies to these suffering people [in West Berlin] this assignment became a worthwhile challenge. But that didn't make this second disruption without some pangs of doubt. However these last feelings of doubt left me when I landed that first load of 20,000 pounds of flour at Tempelhof in West Berlin. The German unloading crew poured through the open cargo door in the back of my aircraft. The lead man came toward the cockpit, moist eyes hand out thrust in friendship. Unintelligible words but his expression said it all. . . . From then on the pangs of doubt were gone.

One day in July 1948 I met 30 kids at the barbed wire fence at Tempelhof in Berlin. They were excited. They said, " When the weather gets so bad you can't land don't worry about us. We can get by on little food but if we lose our freedom we may never get it back." The principle of freedom was more important than the pleasure of enough flour. "Just don't give up on us." they asked. The Soviets had offered the Berliners food rations but they would not capitulate. For the hour I was at the fence not one child asked for gum or candy. Children I had met during and after the war like them in other countries had always begged insistently for such treasures. These Berlin children were so grateful for flour to be free they wouldn't lower themselves to be beggars for something more. It was even the more impressive because they hadn't had gum nor candy for months. When I realized this silent , mature show of gratitude and the strength that it took not to ask, I had to do something. All I had was two sticks of gum. I broke them in two and passed them through the barbed wire. The result was unbelievable. Those with the gum tore off strips of the wrapper and gave them to the others. Those with the strips put them to their noses and smelled the tiny fragrance. The expression of pleasure was unmeasurable. I was so moved by what I saw and their incredible restraint that I promised them I would drop enough gum for each of them the next day as I came over their heads to land. They would know my plane because I would wiggle the wings as I came over the airport. When I got back to Rhein-Main I attached gum and even chocolate bars to three handkerchief parachutes. We wiggled the wings and delivered the goods the next day. What a jubilant celebration. We did the same thing for several weeks before we got caught, threatened with a court martial which was followed immediately by a pardon. General Tunner said, "Keep it up."

1. Discuss the feelings of "doubt" Halvorsen had about this new mission.

2. According to Halvorsen, what seemed to matter most to the West Berliners?

3. Why do you think General Tunner allowed Halvorsen to continue his mission?

Source 3

"The West Can Pull Out of Berlin Proudly," Los Angeles Times, 1948

In 1948, Philip Johnston, a private citizen, wrote a letter to President Truman stating that the Berlin crisis was a result of the President's "incredible stupidity." The solution, Johnston claimed, was clearly stated in an article from the *Los Angeles Times* on September 2. He attached the article to his letter. Here is an excerpt from that article.

Russia Holds Trumps

Russia is holding the trump cards in Berlin and will only give in at a price that may prove too high for the western powers to pay. Besides, any bargain that one may strike with Moscow today by grants of credits, shipment of free goods, acceptance of Communist control of Berlin, elimination of all currency except the Russian-sponsored mark from Berlin, can at best be only temporary. No one expects Stalin to live up to his commitments a month, a week or a day after he has given them. In which case one may well ask, why make the concessions to the Russians in the first place?

The question is more than a diplomatic and political conundrum; it is one of peace and tranquility in Germany and in Europe. . . . Even a most superficial study of the recent activities and attitudes of Russia in Berlin will convince any sensible person that Moscow is staging an intensive effort to drive the western Allies to despair and hence to a declaration of war, in which the Americans, the British, and French will be branded the aggressors. This is a trap that Stalin has set up for the west. . . .

Can Pull Out

The western Allies can pull out of Berlin proudly . . . on the excellent ground that co-operation with Russia is no longer possible. . . . When the westerners have made that decision, they should supplement it with the withdrawal of their ambassadors from Moscow. . . . At the same time the Soviet Ambassadors shall be told that their presence in Washington, London, and Paris is no longer desired. . . . One might object to such a move . . . but it is well to be reminded that for all practical purposes such relations between western powers and Russia have long been nonexistent.

1. According to the writer, are negotiations with Russia possible? Explain.

2. What are the dangers of allowing the blockade to continue?

3. What solution does the writer suggest? What might be an advantage to this solution?

Source 4

Winter Blockade: The First Hundred Days of the Berlin Airlift, October 5, 1948

As the first summer of the Berlin Airlift passed, organizers realized that the coming winter would present new challenges—especially the need for additional coal to heat the city. The following is a report from a special correspondent on the airlift.

October 2 was the hundredth day of the absolute blockade, by land and water of Berlin. Three months ago the joint Anglo-American air-lift was regarded less as a serious operation than as a generous and spontaneous gesture, capable of heartening the German population but certainly not of supplying them with all the essentials of human existence. Three months ago nobody save the small band of planners in British and American headquarters, looked more than a few weeks ahead. The supply of over two million people by air was in summer improbable, in winter unthinkable.

Berlin's needs

In the week before last the air-lift brought over 25.000 tons of food and fuel into Berlin. This gives an average of 3,600 [tons] a day. . . . General Clay, has confidently predicted a 4.500 tons a day average even during the worst winter weather.

What has been the Allied effort to meet these requirements? First they were wise enough to build up substantial stocks. The British are building an unloading dock at Kladow, on Berlin's western girdle of lakes, which will solve the problem of transference from planes to barges. They have organised transit and permanent dumps in the city. They have brought light railways into use for transporting purposes, and at the western end of the air-lift supply services, after a shaky start, are working with an exact, unbroken rhythm.

The first key-point this winter will be the arrival of really cold weather. By then the air-lift will have to be stepped up 40 per cent and a domestic-heating program organized. Coal may have to be withdrawn from industry, but in any case this could not supply more than 25 per cent of needs. Unemployment will then become a menacing problem. The air-lift has proved itself many times over but not yet guaranteed Western Berlin's survival.

---

1. Describe the early reactions to the proposed airlift.

2. What is needed for the airlift to be successful during the winter months?

3. What are the writer's predictions for the success of the airlift? Why?

Lesson 1 The Civil Rights Movement Strengthens

CLOSE READING

Segregation Limits Equality

1. **Draw Inferences** Why is it that "separate but equal" facilities were rarely actually equal?

2. **Identify Supporting Details** The text argues that the de facto segregation in the North had a severe impact on people of color. Give an example of de facto segregation and explain its impact.

A Landmark Supreme Court Decision

3. **Compare and Contrast** How were the goals of CORE and the NAACP similar? How were the organizations different?

4. **Cite Evidence** Explain what methods the NAACP used to gain rights for African Americans. Were these methods successful? Cite evidence to argue why or why not.

Conflict Between Federal and State Power

5. **Analyze Style and Rhetoric** How did Eisenhower attempt to persuade people to stop their actions toward the African American students in his "Address on Little Rock"? Cite specific persuasive words or phrases.

6. **Summarize** Explain how the Little Rock crisis showed the struggle between state and federal governments.

The Montgomery Bus Boycott

7. **Analyze Sequence** What chain of events led to the Montgomery bus boycott?

8. **Draw Inferences** How did Martin Luther King, Jr., harness the power of the African American church community?

Lesson 2 The Movement Surges Forward

CLOSE READING

Student Activists Promote Civil Rights

1. **Identify Cause and Effect** As you read this lesson, take note of important events that led to the passage of the Civil Rights Act of 1964. Use the graphic organizer below to identify cause and effect.

Cause	Effect

Freedom Rides Begin Throughout the South

2. **Summarize** What did the freedom riders hope to accomplish?

3. **Draw Conclusions** Did President Kennedy react to the battles over civil rights in the way most voters expected? Give evidence for your answer.

Public Institutions Open Doors to Minorities

4. Analyze Interactions of People and Events Why did the James Meredith case result in a riot?

Thousands Descend on the Nation's Capital

5. Cite Evidence Why was the March on Washington effective? Cite evidence from the text as you explain.

A Significant Congressional Vote Addresses Minority Rights

6. Identify Cause and Effect Which provision of the Civil Rights Act of 1964 had the potential to make the biggest difference in bringing about greater equality for African Americans? Why? Use details from the text to support your answer.

7. Draw Conclusions What made the civil rights movement successful? Identify at least two people or organizations that contributed to the success of the movement. Explain why these people or organizations were important, using evidence from the text.

Lesson 3 Successes and Setbacks

CLOSE READING

Increasing Participation in the Political Process

1. **Identify Cause and Effect** Why didn't the federal court decisions passed through 1964 have a greater effect on African Americans' right to vote in the South? Use details from the text to support your answer.

2. **Compare and Contrast** Freedom Summer with the Selma March. What were the goals of the people who participated in the events? What kind of opposition did they face? How did they react to the opposition they encountered?

Violence Troubles Civil Rights Efforts

3. **Draw Inferences** Even with the passage of the Voting Rights Act of 1965, racial violence erupted in American cities. What does this suggest about the United States at this time? Use details from the text to support your answer.

4. **Cite Evidence** Are the recommendations of the Kerner Commission still relevant today? Explain why or why not, and cite evidence.

New Civil Rights Groups

5. Summarize In what way was Malcolm X's approach to civil rights different from approaches taken by earlier leaders? Use details from the text to support your answer.

6. Draw Conclusions In what way was Stokely Carmichael's idea of "Black Power" a positive message? In what way did it have a negative effect? Overall, do you think its effect at the time was more positive or more negative? Use details from the text to support your answer.

King Expands His Dream

7. Analyze Interactions Among Individuals and Events How was the assassination of Robert F. Kennedy linked to the assassination of Martin Luther King, Jr.?

Results of the Civil Rights Movement

8. Assess an Argument The text gives reasons why people are both for and against affirmative action. Do you think affirmative action a good idea? Why or why not? Use details from the text to support your answer.

Lesson 4 Kennedy's Reforms

CLOSE READING

The Torch Is Passed to a New Generation

1. **Compare and Contrast** How were Kennedy and Nixon alike? How were they different? Use the Venn diagram below to record your answers.

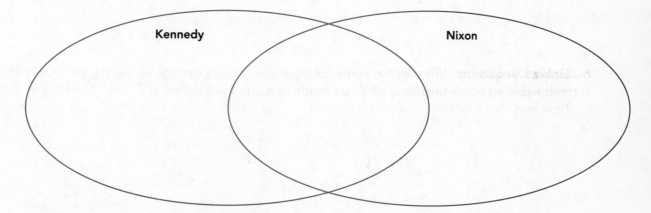

Kennedy   Nixon

2. **Identify Cause and Effect** What factors helped Kennedy win the election of 1960? Give at least two examples, and explain the effect of each.

A President's Unique Charisma

3. **Analyze Style and Rhetoric** What words and phrases did Kennedy use to persuade people to support his policy of the "New Frontier"? Why might his rhetoric have appealed to people of the time? Cite evidence from primary sources.

Domestic Priorities

4. Summarize Explain John F. Kennedy's economic policy. Was it effective?

5. Analyze Sequence Why was Kennedy cautious about supporting civil rights, especially at the beginning of his presidency? What made him change his views?

6. Analyze Interactions Among Events How did the launch of *Sputnik 1* by the Soviet Union lead to the space race? Cite specific events and explain their interactions.

Kennedy Is Assassinated

7. Identify Supporting Details The text states that when Kennedy was killed "it seemed as if part of America's innocence had died with him." What details in the text support this idea? Do you agree or disagree? Why?

Lesson 5 Reform Under Johnson

CLOSE READING

Johnson's Path to the Presidency

1. **Analyze Sequence** What events in Johnson's early life shaped his belief of how the presidency should be? Describe the events in the order in which they occurred.

2. **Compare and Contrast** Compare Lyndon B. Johnson and Barry Goldwater and their views about the role of the federal government.

Creating the Great Society

3. **Determine Central Ideas** Use the chart below to identify key programs in Lyndon B. Johnson's Great Society.

The Great Society

Education	Healthcare	Immigration	Poverty
•	•	•	•

4. **Analyze Style and Rhetoric** What words and phrases did Lyndon B. Johnson use to persuade people to imagine his "Great Society"? Why might these words have appealed to his audience?

5. **Summarize** Why did President Johnson see the need for a new law about immigration? What was the goal of the new law? What were the long-term effects of the law?

6. **Assess an Argument** Choose one of the Great Society programs mentioned in the text and cite evidence as you argue whether it was successful or not.

The Impact of the Warren Court

7. **Identify Cause and Effect** Why was it necessary for the electoral districts to be redrawn in the 1960s? What did the Warren Court do to fix this problem?

8. **Draw Conclusions** Explain the impact of the *Tinker* v. *Des Moines School District* decision. Why was this decision significant? How might it affect schools or free speech today? Give an example.

PRIMARY SOURCE EXPLORATION

Women During the Civil Rights Movement

Introduction

During the civil rights movement of the 1950s and 1960s, African Americans fought for desegregation of public places. They worked toward registering to vote without intimidation from white supremacists. Under the direction of Martin Luther King, Jr. and other leaders, the movement used strategies of nonviolent resistance to achieve its goals. Women were an integral part of the civil rights movement from its beginning. They participated in marches and led boycotts, freedom rides, and voter registration drives. Working toward any kind of integration risked arrest, severe mistreatment, and sometimes death. Yet, African American men and women and their supporters continued their struggle and with great perseverance, won many of the rights they were entitled to as American citizens.

Document-Based Writing Activity

Analyze the following four sources and then use information from the documents and your knowledge of American history to write an essay in which you

- Evaluate the struggles of the civil rights movement.
- Describe the contributions of women to the movement.

Keep in mind that your essay should include an introduction, several paragraphs, and a conclusion. In the body of the essay, use evidence from at least three documents. Support your response with relevant facts, examples, and details. In developing your essay, be sure to keep these general definitions in mind:

- *Evaluate* means "to examine and judge the significance, worth, or condition of; to determine the value of."
- *Describe* means "to illustrate something in words or tell about it."

Source 1

Letter from Women's Political Council to Mayor W.J. Gayle, May 21, 1954

In a letter to the mayor of Montgomery, Alabama, Jo Ann Robinson described the changes African Americans wanted to see from the Montgomery bus system. Robinson was president of the Women's Political Council, an organization that fought for equality for African Americans.

Dear Sir:

The Women's Political Council is very grateful to you and the City Commissioners for the hearing you allowed our representative during the month of March 1954, when the "city-bus-fare-increase case" was being reviewed. There were several things the Council asked for:

1. A city law that would make it possible for Negroes to sit from back toward front, and whites from front toward back until all the seats are taken.

2. That Negroes not be asked or forced to pay fare at front and go to the rear of the bus to enter.

3. That busses stop at every corner in residential sections occupied by Negroes as they do in communities where whites reside.

We are happy to report that busses have begun stopping at more corners now in some sections where Negroes live than previously. However, the same practices in seating and boarding the bus continue.

Mayor Gayle, three-fourths of the riders of these public conveyances [vehicles] are Negroes. If Negroes did not patronize [utilize or support] them, they could not possibly operate. . . .

There has been talk from twenty-five or more local organizations of planning a city-wide boycott of busses. . . .

Please consider this plea, and if possible, act favorably upon it, for even now plans are being made to ride less, or not at all, on our busses. We do not want this.

Respectfully yours,
The Women's Political Council
Jo Ann Robinson, President

1. What changes does Jo Ann Robinson ask Mayor Gayle and the City Commissioners to make to the Montgomery bus system?

2. "Leverage" is a word that means "to use something to its maximum advantage." What leverage does Robinson use with the mayor?

3. How do you think Mayor Gayle responded to Jo Ann Robinson's letter?

Source 2

Freedom Riders Speak for Themselves, News & Letters, November 1961

Freedom Rides through the Deep South began in 1961 to test a 1960 Supreme Court ruling that banned segregation in interstate transportation facilities. African American and white Freedom Riders were arrested in Jackson, Mississippi, for using a white-only waiting area. Freedom Rider Mary Hamilton told what it was like to spend time in the Hinds County Jail.

After our trial we were transferred to Hinds County Jail. It is right across the street from the City Jail. Crossing the street, we sang "We Shall Overcome," the beautiful theme song of the Freedom Rider movement. The jailers told us if we didn't stop singing we were going to find things very difficult. They shouted at us and threatened us. We continued singing as we crossed the street.

We were herded into a very small room with our luggage. Then we were split up into Negro and white, and told to follow some plainclothes policemen [a police officer not wearing a uniform]. We began to sing our theme song, "We Shall Overcome." We were told to shut up. We sang louder and louder. The officials told us we were just making it harder on ourselves.

Upstairs, we were told to put our suitcases down and pick up a bedroll [rolled up bedding]. We weren't allowed to take any personal things like wash cloths or toothbrushes. We were told we'd get them that night. We didn't.

The cell was about 15 x 15 feet. It had a shower stall and a toilet, all completely open. There were two barred windows at the top, and four steel bunks. When we entered, we found two other girls already there, one from Atlanta and one from Los Angeles. White girls were in one cell, and Negro girls in another. Everyone cheered as we came in. . . .

We were not allowed visits from anyone. A Negro minister visited us once, but was permitted to talk only to Negro girls. The white girls tried to talk to him, but he evidently felt it too dangerous to talk to them. . . .

The other inmates did as much for us as they could—buy things for us and exchange notes between Freedom Riders. The fellows were down at another end. In the evening we sang to each other. The fellows sang first, and we answered. All day we looked forward to notes passed between the fellows and the girls. Our morale was high.

---

1. What did Mary Hind say the Freedom Riders did on their way to jail? Why do you think they did this?

2. What conditions did the Freedom Riders face after they were sent to jail?

3. Why do you think the other inmates helped the Freedom Riders?

Source 3

Speech Before the Credentials Committee, Democratic National Convention, Fannie Lou Hamer, August 22, 1964

At the Democratic National Convention, Fannie Lou Hamer sought to make the Mississippi Freedom Democratic Party (MFDP), which represented African Americans, the official Mississippi delegation. That is because the state's official delegation did not include any Black Mississippians. Although her efforts did not succeed, Hamer gave inspirational testimony.

And June the 9th, 1963, I had attended a voter registration workshop; was returning back to Mississippi. Ten of us was traveling by the Continental Trailway bus. When we got to Winona, Mississippi, . . . four of the people got off to use the washroom, and two of the people—to use the restaurant. . . .

The four people that had gone in to use the restaurant was ordered out. During this time I was on the bus. But when I looked through the window and saw they had rushed out I got off the bus to see what had happened. And one of the ladies said, "it was a State Highway Patrolman and a Chief of Police ordered us out." I got back on the bus and one of the persons had used the washroom got back on the bus, too.

As soon as I was seated on the bus, I saw when they began to get the five people in a highway patrolman's car. I stepped off of the bus to see what was happening and somebody screamed from the car that the five workers was in and said, "Get that one there." And when I went to get in the car, when the man told me I was under arrest, he kicked me. . . .

After I was placed in the cell I began to hear sounds of licks [beatings] and screams, I could hear the sounds of licks and horrible screams. . . .

And it wasn't too long before three white men came to my cell. One of these men was a State Highway Patrolman and he asked me where I was from, and told him Ruleville. He said, "We are going to check this."

And they left my cell and it wasn't too long before they came back. He said, "You're from Ruleville all right," and he used a curse word. And he said, "We're going to make you wish you was dead.". . .

All of this on account of we want to register, to become first-class citizens.

1. Why did Fannie Lou Hamer want to speak at the Democratic National Convention?

2. Why do you think Hamer decided to tell this story?

3. How does Fannie Lou Hamer's description of jail compare to Mary Hamilton's in Source 2?

Source 4

Selma to Montgomery March, 1965

The image below captures a moment of the five day 54-mile walk from Selma to Montgomery, Alabama. The participants included men and women, African Americans, and whites. People from all over the United States joined the march—from Los Angeles to Kansas City.

1. How would you describe the expressions on most of the marchers faces?

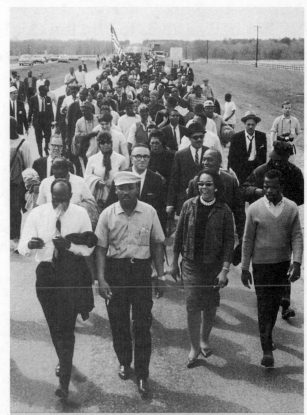

Martin Luther King, Jr. and his wife Coretta Scott King [center] led the march from Selma to Montgomery, Alabama.

2. Look far into the distance of the image and you may notice that someone is carrying an American flag. Why do you think the marchers carried American flags?

3. Why do you think the photographer who took this picture took it from this angle? What did the photographer want to show?

Lesson 1 The Cold War and Vietnam

CLOSE READING

Kennedy Strives to Win the Cold War

1. **Analyze Sequence** How was Kennedy's foreign policy a reaction to the Eisenhower years?

2. **Identify Cause and Effect** Why did Kennedy initiate programs such as the Peace Corps and the Alliance for Progress that reached out to Third World nations?

Kennedy Responds to Communism in Cuba

3. **Identify Cause and Effect** Why did the United States plan the Bay of Pigs invasion of Cuba? Explain the results of the invasion.

4. **Determine Meaning of Words and Phrases** What did Secretary of State Dean Rusk mean when he said, "eyeball to eyeball, they blinked first"?

The Causes and Outcomes of the Berlin Crisis

5. **Analyze Interactions Among People and Events** Describe how the conflict between Khrushchev and Kennedy at the conference in Vienna led to the construction of the Berlin Wall.

Reasons for U.S. Involvement in Indochina

6. **Analyze Sequence** What led Vietnamese nationalists to fight for independence from France after World War II? What effects did this struggle have through 1954? Use this chart to record your answers.

Causes

Vietnamese Fight for Independence

Effects

The United States Responds to Communism in Vietnam

7. **Identify Steps in a Process** How did the United States first become involved with Ngo Dinh Diem's government? What actions did the United States take to escalate its involvement?

8. **Evaluate Explanations** Did President Johnson's actions in response to the Gulf of Tonkin incident show a "monolithic" view of communism? Explain why or why not.

Lesson 2 America's Role Escalates

CLOSE READING

Escalation of Forces in Vietnam

1. **Compare and Contrast** Compare U.S. involvement in the Vietnam War before and after the Gulf of Tonkin Resolution.

2. **Paraphrase** Ho Chi Minh explained that his Vietcong guerillas fought like a tiger against an elephant. Explain this simile in your own words, and then come up with your own comparison that describes how the Vietnamese and American forces fought.

3. **Cite Evidence** A stated goal of the Vietnam War was to win the "hearts and minds" of the Vietnamese people. Did American tactics support this goal? Cite evidence as you make your argument.

Patriotism, Heroism, and Sinking Morale

4. **Analyze Interactions Among People and Events** Why did the United States have to use different strategies and tactics in Vietnam than those it had used successfully in World War II?

5. Identify Supporting Details What hardships did American nurses face in Vietnam?

6. Identify Explanations Use this flowchart to identify three reasons why American servicemembers supported the war effort and three reasons why they questioned the cause up through the mid-1960s.

Soldiers' Views of the War

Support the War

Question the War

Doubt Grows on the Home Front

7. Identify Cause and Effect How did Johnson's policies in the Vietnam War affect his Great Society policies? What other events or trends affected both of these policies?

8. Draw Inferences Lyndon B. Johnson was a Democrat. How do you think the tension between conservative "hawks" and liberal "doves" affected his political power?

Lesson 3 The Antiwar Movement

CLOSE READING

Antiwar Sentiment Grows

1. **Identify Supporting Details** Why were poorer men disproportionately drafted during the Vietnam War? Use evidence from the text to support your answer.

2. **Analyze Interactions Among People and Events** How did the civil rights movement interact with the antiwar movement? Use evidence from the text to support your answer.

3. **Identify Cause and Effect** How did the media coverage of the Vietnam War affect people's perceptions of the war? Use evidence from the text to support your answer.

The Tet Offensive

4. **Cite Evidence** Why was the United States military surprised by the Tet Offensive? Cite evidence from the text to support your answer.

5. Identify Cause and Effect Fill out the chart below with some effects of the Tet Offensive.

Military Effects	Effects on Views of the War

The 1968 Presidential Race

6. Draw Conclusions What led to the riots surrounding the Democratic National Convention in Chicago in 1968? Use evidence from the text to support your answer.

7. Identify Supporting Details Identify and explain at least two strategies that allowed Richard Nixon to win the election of 1968.

Lesson 4 The War's End and Effects

CLOSE READING

Attempts to Withdraw from Vietnam

1. **Draw Inferences** Why was Nixon's goal of "peace with honor" so difficult to achieve? Use details from the text to support your answer.

2. **Identify the Meaning of Words and Phrases** What was "Vietnamization?" What was the Nixon's goal in pursuing this policy?

Events Intensify the Antiwar Movement

3. **Analyze Style and Rhetoric** What emotionally charged language did Richard Nixon use to persuade people that going into Cambodia was the right thing to do?

4. **Summarize** What happened in the Vietnamese village of My Lai that shocked Americans at home?

The Vietnam War Ends

5. Sequence What events followed the signing of the Paris Peace Accords in 1973?

6. Draw Conclusions Who won the war in Vietnam? Who lost? Support your answer with evidence from the text.

Effects of the Vietnam War

7. Identify Cause and Effect Use this outline to list some of the effects of the Vietnam War

I. Effects on Southeast Asia
   A.

II. Effects on American Veterans
   A.

III. Effects on US Policy and Economy
   A.

PRIMARY SOURCE EXPLORATION

Reactions to the Vietnam War

Introduction

Do you remember why the United States entered World War II? You should! It was a dramatic and pivotal moment. Japanese planes launched a surprise attack on the United States Navy at Pearl Harbor, killing thousands and enraging the nation.

Compare that to the Vietnam War. Then, there was no surprise attack on American soil. Instead, the United States escalated its involvement in a foreign conflict conflict slowly, over several years.

Now consider how the two wars ended. In 1945, American troops occupied Germany and Japan. But in 1975, it was America's communist opponents who were victorious, taking control of South Vietnam after the United States withdrew its troops.

So it is perhaps not surprising that Americans viewed the two wars very differently. In the primary sources that follow, you will study Americans' reactions to these two conflicts.

Document-Based Writing Activity

Analyze the following four sources and then use information from the documents and your knowledge of American history to write an essay in which you

- Compare and contrast Americans' responses to World War II and the Vietnam War.
- Discuss why the Vietnam War was more divisive than World War II.

Keep in mind that your essay should include an introduction, several paragraphs, and a conclusion. In the body of the essay, use evidence from at least three documents. Support your response with relevant facts, examples, and details. In developing your essay, be sure to keep these general definitions in mind:

- *Compare and contrast* means "to examine things and see how they are both similar and different."
- *Discuss* means "to make observations about something using facts, reasoning, and argument; to present in some detail."

Source 1

"Meet the Girls Who Keep 'Em Flying," Frank J. Taylor, *Saturday Evening Post*, 1942

After the Japanese attack on Pearl Harbor on December 7, 1941, Americans joined the war effort in huge numbers. Some volunteered to fight while others took jobs in factories that produced materials needed by the military. This 1942 article includes interviews with women who took jobs in an aircraft factory.

Fuming [furious] over the sneak bombing of Pearl Harbor, Mrs. Clover Hoffman, diminutive [small] and spirited mother of Cliff and Charlotte, twins aged 3½, reached a decision important in the task of defeating the [Japanese] and the Nazis. Resigning her job as waitress in a San Diego restaurant, and parking the twins with her mother, Mrs. Hoffman presented herself at the employment office of the Consolidated Aircraft Corporation. "I want to work on a bomber," she told Mrs. Mamie Kipple, assistant employment director in charge of hiring the women who work in the company's two sprawling plants.

"Why do you want to work on a bomber?" asked Mrs. Kipple.

"That's something I can do to help bring Harry back."

"Who is Harry?"

"My husband. He's machinist's mate [a naval job] on a destroyer at Pearl Harbor."

"Have you ever worked in a factory?"

"No; but I can learn, if you'll give me a chance."

1. How does Mamie Kipple feel about the attack on Pearl Harbor?

2. What does Kipple do in reaction to the attack? How did it affect her personally?

3. What do Kipple's experiences tell you about the way ordinary American civilians participated in World War II?

Source 2

We Refuse to Serve, 1967

The flyer quoted below was created by an anti-war group during the Vietnam War. It used strong language to encourage young men to resist the draft, calling the war not only unjustified but "criminal."

In the past few months, in many parts of the country, a resistance has been forming. . . A resistance of young men – joined together in their commitment against the war. . .

We will renounce all deferments and refuse to cooperate with the draft in any manner, at any level. We have taken this stand for varied reasons:

- opposition to conscription

- opposition only to the Viet Nam war

- opposition to all wars and to all American military adventures.

We all agree on one point: the War in Viet Nam is criminal and we must act together, at great individual risk, to stop it. Those involved must lead the American people, by their example, to understand the enormity of what their government is doing. . . . . that the government cannot be allowed to continue with its daily crimes. . . .

There are many ways to avoid the draft, to stay clear of this war. Most of us now have deferments . . . but all these individual outs can have no effect on the draft, the war or the consciousness of this country. To cooperate with conscription is to perpetuate its existence, without which, the government could not wage war. We have chosen to openly defy the draft and confront the government and its war directly.

This is no small decision in a person's life. Each one realizes that refusing to cooperate with [the draft] may mean prison. Again we agree that to do anything but this is to effectively abet [aid] the war. The government will not be permitted to use us on its way to greater crimes and destruction. We prefer to resist.

---

1. The flyer lists three types of opposition to the draft. How are they different?

2. Why might the writers of this flyer believe that the war effort is "criminal?"

3. What specifically are the writers of this flyer calling on young men to do? What risk would those young men be taking?

Source 3

Photograph of a Protest March in Cleveland, Ohio, 1965

Many opponents of the Vietnam War, like those pictured here, questioned the drafting of African Americans to fight for a country that often treated them poorly. They also argued that the draft system was unfair to African Americans, who died at higher rates in Vietnam than white soldiers.

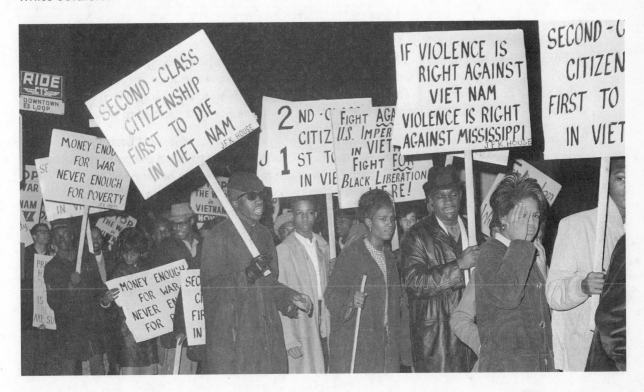

1. Rephrase the sign "SECOND-CLASS CITIZENSHIP; FIRST TO DIE IN VIETNAM" in your own words.

2. Another sign reads "MONEY ENOUGH FOR WAR, NEVER ENOUGH FOR POVERTY." Why do you think the protesters connected these two things?

3. Why do you think similar protests did not occur during World War II, even though the military was officially segregated at that time?

Source 4

Account by Marine Volunteer Richard Houser, 2003

Despite an active and vocal anti-war movement, many young men volunteered for service in Vietnam, far more than were ever drafted. This account gives one young volunteer's perspective.

When we discussed the Vietnam War there were times when neither of us was going, there were times when both of us were going, there were times when Nathan [the author's brother] was going and I wasn't, and there were times when I was going and he wasn't. The question we were wrestling with was, what do you owe your country? I finally came to the conclusion that even if the war wasn't the best thing to be doing, which we kind of thought it wasn't, as long as I was going to live in the States, I needed to serve.

It wasn't anything noble, or honorable, from my vantage point. Part of it was I probably didn't want to embarrass Dad. Anyway, I decided if I wasn't ready to leave the country and they were going to be in this thing, I might as well get it over with. I've never been good at waiting for things to happen. And if I'm going to do it, I thought I might as well go with what we thought was the toughest branch and join the Marine Corps.

I had no question I was going to Vietnam. I volunteered. I also volunteered for a seven-month extension in Vietnam after my first tour. I got in-country in 1966 and left in 1968. I was in avionics with the 56th Marine Air Wing. We kept all the radios, radar, and electrical equipment for the aircraft in working order. I also volunteered as a crew member on helicopters.

1. What is Houser's opinion about the war in Vietnam?

2. What reasons does Houser give for enlisting?

3. Compare this letter to Source 1. How are the sentiments expressed in the two accounts different?

Lesson 1 The Counterculture of the 1960s

CLOSE READING

A Counterculture Emerges

1. **Paraphrase** Explain how the quote from Jerry Rubin illustrates the generation gap of the 1960s.

2. **Compare and Contrast** Compare and contrast the environments in which the baby boomers and their parents grew up. Include information about major events and how those events impacted each generation.

3. **Use Visual Information** Analyze the photograph of a hippie wedding, which shows a young man and woman embracing in unconventional wedding clothes. What values were important to these people? Use information from both the text and the photograph to support your ideas.

4. **Determine Central Ideas** Use the web diagram below to give examples of the main ideas of the counterculture. Include information about how the counterculture distinguished itself through music, politics, education, media, and personal style.

Counterculture

The Counterculture Shapes a Generation

5. Draw Inferences What did the music and the art of the 1960s have in common? Make connections between at least one musician and one artist of the time.

6. Draw Conclusions What criticism do you think the Haight-Ashbury district of San Francisco drew? Make connections to ways people criticize people with alternate lifestyles today.

7. Draw Inferences Why did the ideas of Buddhism and other eastern religions, as well as the values of the Native Americans, appeal to members of the hippie counterculture?

8. Summarize What events contributed to the end of the counterculture movement of the 1960s?

Lesson 2 The Women's Rights Movement

CLOSE READING

A New Feminist Movement Pushes for Equality

1. **Analyze Sequence** What events in the 1940s, 1950s, and 1960s led to the need for a second wave of feminism?

2. **Summarize** Why did some leaders of the feminist movement use the phrase "Jane Crow" to motivate people to act?

3. **Analyze Style and Rhetoric** What aspects of the excerpt from *The Feminine Mystique* by Betty Friedan made her writing particularly powerful? Give examples.

The Role of Women's Civil Rights Organizations

4. **Assess an Argument** Charlotte Bunch wrote that "there is no private domain of a person's life that is not political and there is no political issue that is not ultimately personal." Do you agree? Use evidence from the texts about women's rights to support your answer.

5. **Explain an Argument** Phyllis Schlafly argued that the Equal Rights Amendment was harmful to American families. Explain and summarize Schlafly's beliefs.

The Impact of the Women's Movement

6. **Identify Cause and Effect** Title IX required colleges to have better opportunities for women in athletics. What mixed consequences did this have?

7. **Identify Cause and Effect** What hidden causes led to women getting paid less than men?

8. **Analyze Interactions** Explain the relationship between the "pink-collar ghetto" and the feminization of poverty.

Lesson 3 Expanding the Push for Equality

CLOSE READING

Latino Immigration Surges

1. **Identify Cause and Effect** What events and trends led Latino immigrants to leave their home countries and come to the United States?

2. **Draw Inferences** The Immigration and Nationality Act was passed in 1965, and it eliminated quotas for immigrants, allowing many more Latino immigrants to come into the United States. What other events in the United States might have led to the passage of this law?

Latino Organizations Fight for Rights

3. **Draw Conclusions** How was Cesar Chavez influenced by Dr. King and the Civil Rights Movement?

4. **Compare and Contrast** What similarities and differences do you see between the Chicano movement and the Harlem Renaissance?

American Indians and Asian Americans Battle Discrimination

5. **Determine Central Idea** Analyze the excerpt from Dee Brown's influential book, *Bury My Heart at Wounded Knee.* What is Brown's central idea? Explain it in your own words.

6. **Compare and Contrast** Compare and contrast the goals of the Japanese American Citizens League and the American Indian Movement.

Rights for Consumers and the Disabled

7. **Make Inferences** If Franklin D. Roosevelt had shown his disability openly, do you think rights for people with disabilities would have been achieved earlier? Explain your answer using evidence.

The Gay Rights Movement Advances

8. **Draw Conclusions** Why do you think the post-Stonewall tactic of LGBT people coming out to friends, families, and co-workers achieved such dramatic results?

Lesson 4 The Environmental Movement

CLOSE READING

Environmental Activists Sound the Alarm

1. **Analyze Sequence** Use the sequence graphic organizer to record the major events that led up to the environmental movement. Include information about what year each event occurred.

2. **Draw Inferences** What can you infer about Rachel Carson's writing style in *Silent Spring*? Explain your inference.

3. **Analyze Author's Point of View** Based on the quote that the Cuyahoga River "oozes, rather than flows," and that a person "does not drown but decays," what can you conclude about point of view of the author of the article in *Time* magazine about the fire?

4. **Draw Conclusions** What conclusions can you draw about the public sentiment toward the environment in the 1960s, based on the laws Nixon passed as president? Cite evidence to support your conclusions.

Impact of Environmental Regulations

5. **Identify Supporting Details** What details from either primary or secondary sources were most effective in helping you understand the toxic chemicals in Love Canal in New York?

6. **Draw Inferences** Why did the events at Three Mile Island delay the development of nuclear energy for such a long time?

7. **Summarize** What were some of the arguments against environmental regulations? Explain at least two arguments in your own words.

8. **Use Visual Information** Study the map of Superfund Sites in "Impact of Environmental Regulations." Which regions of the country might have the most pollution from nineteenth-century industry?

Lesson 5 The Two Sides of the Nixon Presidency

CLOSE READING

Nixon's New Approach to Foreign Policy

1. Draw Inferences What message did Nixon send by choosing Henry Kissinger as his key advisor on national security and international affairs?

Opening Relations With China

2. Identify Supporting Details Why did Nixon change his position against China and choose to recognize it as a country? Give at least three reasons.

Nixon's Policy of Détente

3. Compare and Contrast How was Nixon's Cold War diplomacy different from that of his predecessors? Why?

Nixon's Domestic Policy

4. Draw Inferences How did Richard Nixon's defeats in the 1960 presidential race and the 1962 race for governor of California shape his policy as president?

5. **Summarize** Explain why oil prices affected the U.S. economy in the 1970s.

Nixon's "Southern Strategy"

6. **Explain an Argument** Why did people oppose court-ordered busing? Why was Nixon's stance on this issue especially appealing to blue-collar workers and southern whites?

The Watergate Scandal Brings Nixon Down

7. **Paraphrase** In your own words, explain why the U.S. Supreme Court ordered Nixon to release the White House tapes. Use the excerpt from the *United States v. Nixon* decision, written by Burger, as a source.

8. **Identify Cause and Effect** Use the graphic organizer below to explain the effects of Nixon's resignation and the Watergate scandal. Include at least two effects.

Cause	Effect
Richard Nixon resigns because of the Watergate scandal.	

Lesson 6 Ford and Carter Struggle

CLOSE READING

Ford Governs Through Difficult Times

1. **Use Visual Information** Use the photo in "Ford Governs Through Difficult Times" that shows a crowd opposing Ford's pardoning of Nixon, as well as information from the text to explain why the public was so upset when Ford pardoned Nixon.

Ford Continues Nixon's Foreign Policies

2. **Draw Conclusions** Why didn't the United States intervene in the Khmer Rouge genocide?

A New President Faces Challenges

3. **Summarize** What were the advantages and disadvantages of Jimmy Carter being an "outsider" with little previous experience in politics?

Foreign Policy Changes Under Carter

4. **Compare and Contrast** How was Carter's foreign policy similar to and different from Nixon's foreign policy?

Success and Setback in the Middle East

5. Identify Cause and Effect Why did the United States support the Shah's rule in Iran from the 1950s to the 1970s? Why did this support cause anger among many Iranians?

6. Draw Inferences Why were 66 Americans taken hostage during the Iranian Revolution?

Unease Over Changing Values

7. Identify Supporting Details What factors drew people to the Sunbelt of the South and West during the 1970s? Identify a few examples.

8. Cite Evidence Why did fundamentalist and evangelical Christianity experience a resurgence in the 1970s? Use Jerry Falwell's quote and other information in the text as evidence.

PRIMARY SOURCE EXPLORATION

Native Americans Fight for Their Rights

Introduction

For centuries, Native Americans faced the growing power of colonists and settlers who forced them off their lands and onto reservations where they suffered from high rates of poverty and unemployment. In dealing with native peoples, for many years the United States government pursued a policy of assimilation, in an attempt to eliminate any cultural differences between Native Americans and the majority of the population. However, inspired by the civil rights movement, in the 1970s various Native American groups began fighting for their rights.

Document-Based Writing Activity

Analyze the following four sources and then use information from the documents and your knowledge of United States history to write an essay in which you

- Describe the problems that Native Americans faced within the United States.
- Discuss how Native Americans fought for and achieved some of their goals in the 1970s.

Keep in mind that your essay should include an introduction, several paragraphs, and a conclusion. In the body of the essay, use evidence from at least three documents. Support your response with relevant facts, examples, and details. In developing your essay, be sure to keep these general definitions in mind:

- *Describe* means "to illustrate something in words or tell about it."
- *Discuss* means "to make observations about something using facts, reasoning, and argument; to present in some detail."

Source 1

Photo of the occupation of Alcatraz by the Indians of All Tribes (IOAT), 1969

In late 1969, a group of Native American activists and their supporters occupied Alcatraz, an island in the San Francisco Bay that had once been used as a federal prison. The group called themselves the Indians of All Tribes and demanded the creation of a Native American cultural center on the island. In the proclamation they made at the beginning of their occupation, leaders of the movement stated: "We, the Native Americans, reclaim this land known as Alcatraz Island in the name of all American Indians by right of discovery. . . . We will purchase said Alcatraz Island for $24 in glass beads, a precedent set by White Man's purchase of a single island about three hundred years ago. . . "

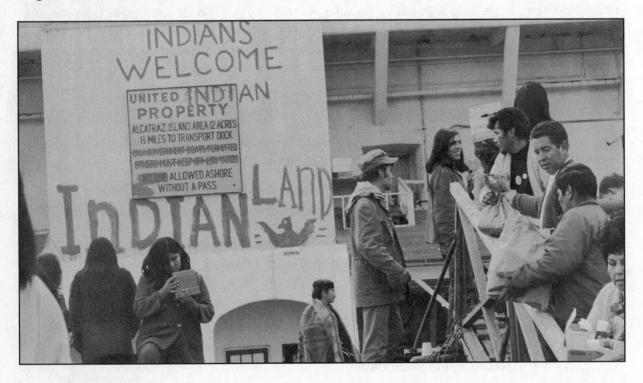

1. What other famous purchase of an island in American history is the speaker referring to?

2. In what ways does the graffiti express the goals and viewpoints of the Native American protesters?

3. What is happening on the gangplank at the far right of the photo?

Source 2

Excerpt from the National Council on Indian Opportunity newsletter

Native American political activism yielded results under President Nixon. In this article, John C. Rainer, a Taos Pueblo Indian, describes the battle to preserve sacred Indian lands in New Mexico.

Self-Determination is the Answer

For decades, the Indian people have struggled to gain a responsive audience in Washington to their voices of dissatisfaction with Federal Indian policies. But, in spite of these efforts, the full scale hearing had eluded us. . . until recently. The 48,000 acres of sacred Indian lands at and near Blue Lake in New Mexico is a dramatic case in point. The United States Government wrote a bitter page in Indian history when it expropriated these lands to create a national forest in 1906. Since that time we have fought to restore rightful possession of this holy lake and watershed area to our people.

These holy lands are a symbol of all religious and territorial rights of Indians everywhere. And now, as we rally our forces for the current push to regain our ceremonial lands, President Nixon has provided us with strong personal support through his legislative proposals.

When the legislation endorsed by the President in his message of July 8, 1970 is passed, Taos Pueblo Indians will regain their lands with a trust title, and the American Indian will accomplish his greatest triumph in years. The legislation also will achieve a milestone in Federal relations with Indians but substantially reducing Indian suspicion of the intent of Federal Government policies.

Indian Action and NCIO

In the past, non-Indians always directed Indian affairs at the national level. Now, with the present Administration, the Indians are active participants in the process of Federal policy-making and program formulation.

To assist in implementing the President's desire to increase the Indian-Administration dialogue, Indian members of the Council have been meeting with tribal leaders throughout the country. These NCIO-sponsored meetings have opened up a productive vehicle for involving Indians in assessing and determining legislation.

---

1. According to this account, what did the Federal Government do with the sacred lands in New Mexico in 1906?

2. Why does the writer believe that relations between Indians and the Federal Government are improving?

3. Why do you think Native Americans feel so strongly about land claims?

Source 3

1976 Senate Judiciary Committee Report on Revolutionary Activities Within the American Indian Movement

Despite improving relations between Native Americans and the federal government, the government remained suspicious of many Indian activist groups, such as the American Indian Movement (AIM). Here Senator James Eastland reports to Congress.

We are here today to receive testimony concerning the American Indian Movement. There is no question in the minds of the great majority of Americans that our Indian citizens have many legitimate grievances and that there is much that must be done to eliminate the inequities and improve the quality of their lives. . .

Several years ago there appeared on the scene a new organization, the American Indian Movement, which claimed to speak for the majority of the American Indians. It attracted a lot of public attention, primarily as a result of its violent occupation of the Bureau of Indian Affairs Building in Washington in the month of November 1972 and its occupation of the town of Wounded Knee, South Dakota for a period of 11 weeks beginning in February of 1973. . .

As a result of the extensive publicity the American Indian Movement received from these episodes, the public impression was that the American Indian Movement spoke for the masses of the Indian people. This, of course, is simply not true. The elected tribal councils speak for the masses of the Indian people - and the record is clear that the elected tribal councils look upon the American Indian Movement as a radical and subversive organization.

The purpose of today's hearing is to try to establish whether there is, in fact, reason for believing that the American Indian Movement is a radical subversive organization rather than an organization committed to improving the lot of the American Indians. One of the questions that has to be answered is whether there are any demonstrable ties between the American Indian Movement and the various Communist movements that exist in our country.

1. What does the senator say about Native American grievances?

2. What distinction does he make between the radical groups and the tribal councils?

3. How does the senator attempt to influence his audience's opinion of the radical groups?

Source 4

Photograph of President Richard Nixon signing the Indian Self-Determination and Education Assistance Act of 1975

The Indian Self-Determination and Education Assistance Act of 1975 fulfilled one of the main goals of the American Indian Movement, allowing Indian groups greater control over the resources and education on reservations. In this photo, President Nixon is signing the bill with Indian leaders.

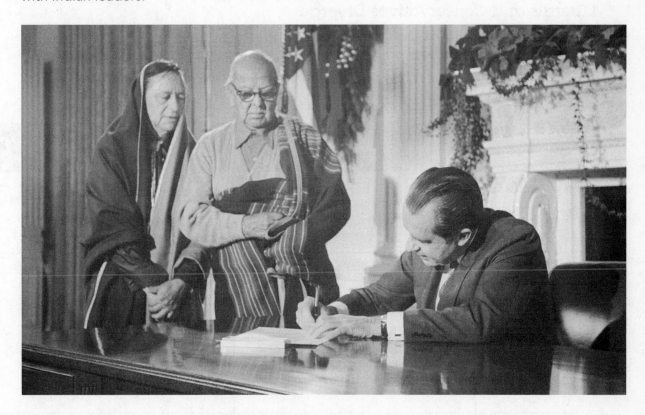

1. Why would control of education on tribal lands be so important to Native Americans?

2. How have the Native American leaders in this photograph chosen to represent Indian culture?

3. Why would the phrase "Self-Determination" be important for Native Americans?

Lesson 1 The Conservative Movement Surges

CLOSE READING

Liberals and Conservatives Diverge

1. **Compare and Contrast** Use the graphic organizer below to take notes about the differences between the liberal and conservative viewpoints in the 1980s. Include information about the economic views, foreign policy, and values associated with each viewpoint.

Issue	Liberals	Conservatives
Economic Views		
Foreign Policy		
Values		

The Increasing Popularity of the New Right

2. **Identify Cause and Effect** What events in the 1960s and 1970s led to a decline in the public's faith in the federal government?

3. **Analyze Interactions Among Events** What migration trends, political events, and demographic patterns contributed to the rise of the Republican Party in the 1980s?

A Conservative Wins the White House

4. **Analyze Style and Rhetoric** Analyze President Reagan's quote from his televised address, "A Time for Choosing." What words does Reagan use to appeal to conservative Americans?

5. **Identify Supporting Details** What political experience did Ronald Reagan have before being elected to the presidency in 1980?

Lesson 2 The Reagan Era

CLOSE READING

A New Direction for the American Economy

1. **Categorize** Use the graphic organizer below to summarize the advantages and disadvantages of President Reagan's policy of supply-side economics.

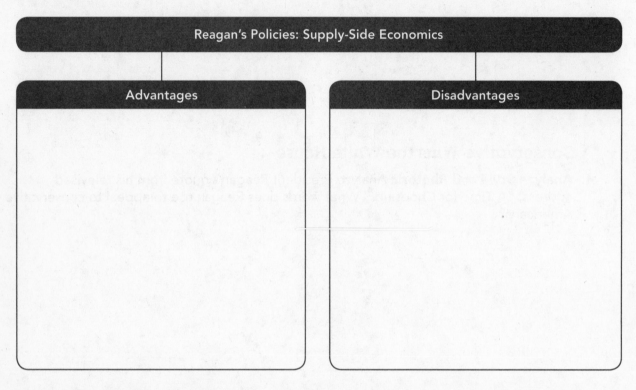

Reagan's Policies: Supply-Side Economics

Advantages

Disadvantages

2. **Identify Supporting Details** What Reagan policies were considered business-friendly? Give examples from the text.

Conservative Momentum Continues

3. Identify Central Ideas What changes did President Reagan make to the Supreme Court during his time in office?

4. Summarize What was the Americans With Disabilities Act?

Culture, Challenge, and Change

5. Summarize What advances happened during the 1980s because of the space program?

6. Explain Name one challenge during Ronald Reagan's presidency and explain how he handled this challenge.

Lesson 3 The Cold War Ends

CLOSE READING

Reagan Leads with "Peace Through Strength"

1. **Summarize** How did President Reagan deal with communist threats in Central and South America?

2. **Identify Supporting Details** What human rights issue did President Reagan encounter during his battle against communism in the 1980s?

3. **Determine Central Ideas** What was President Reagan's central idea in his speech to the students at Moscow State University in 1988? Cite specific words or phrases that might have been particularly inspiring to Reagan's audience.

4. **Use Visual Information** Analyze the photographs of Reagan and Gorbachev in this text. What might these photographs have meant to citizens in both the United States and the Soviet Union?

Impact of the End of the Cold War

5. Paraphrase this quote from *Time* magazine: "It was one of those rare times when the tectonic plates of history shift beneath men's feet."

6. Summarize In what ways were Gorbachev's policies of *glasnost* and *perestroika* successful?

U.S. Involvement in the Middle East and the Iran-Contra Affair

7. Draw Conclusions Why did the Iran-Contra affair anger many people?

8. Identify Supporting Details According to the text, the politics in the Middle East in the 1980s were often complicated and dangerous. Find two pieces of evidence that support this statement.

Lesson 4 A New Era in Foreign Policy

CLOSE READING

Bush Forges a New Role in the World

1. **Summarize** Record events during the Bush presidency for each country below, including the date on which each event occurred.

Foreign Events	
Panama	
China	
South Africa	
Yugoslavia	
Somalia	

2. **Draw Inferences** Why did President Bush respond differently to the crisis in Somalia than he did to the crisis in China?

The Persian Gulf War

3. **Identify Cause and Effect** Explain the reasons why the United States chose to intervene when Iraq invaded Kuwait in 1990.

Clinton Wins the 1992 Election

4. Identify Cause and Effect What factors led Bill Clinton to triumph over President Bush in the 1992 election? Cite at least three causes from the text.

Clinton Intervenes with Mixed Success

5. Summarize How was President Clinton's foreign policy influenced by the Vietnam War? Give an example to support your answer.

America and the Middle East in the 1990s

6. Draw Inferences Why did the United States try to establish peace between Israelis and Palestinians?

Free Trade and Treaties

7. Explain Arguments List the arguments for and against NAFTA.

Lesson 5 Clinton and the 1990s

CLOSE READING

Clinton Enacts New Domestic Policies

1. **Determine Central Ideas** Describe President Clinton's main legislative successes and failures.

2. **Draw Inferences** Consider President Clinton's major legislative goals. What do they reveal about his underlying beliefs about the role of government?

Republicans Lead a Conservative Resurgence

3. **Summarize** On what grounds did Newt Gingrich and his followers attack President Clinton?

4. **Draw Inferences** How did President Clinton react to the Republican resurgence in 1994?

Scandals, Impeachment, and Trial

5. Explain Why was President Clinton investigated twice for his investments in a real estate company and what were the results of those investigations?

6. Summarize the arguments for and against Clinton's impeachment. Use the graphic organizer below to organize your ideas.

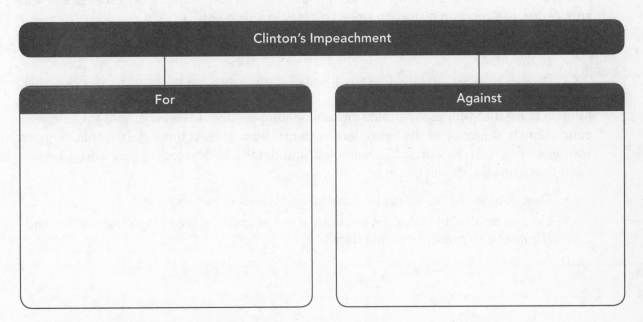

Clinton's Impeachment

For

Against

Digital Technology Changes American Life

7. Analyze Sequence How did historical events earlier in the century impact technology in the 1990s? Give at least two examples.

PRIMARY SOURCE EXPLORATION

Fighting for the Rights of Americans with Disabilities

Introduction

Today we take for granted wheelchair ramps in public buildings, Braille lettering on ATMs, and closed captioning on videos. But this was not always the case. Disabled Americans had to fight for what they needed to live full, productive lives. When President George H.W. Bush signed the Americans With Disabilities Act (ADA) on July 26, 1990, it was a major victory for disabled rights advocates.

Document-Based Writing Activity

Analyze the following four sources and then use information from the documents and your knowledge of American history to write an essay in which you

- Describe the discrimination and challenges faced by disabled Americans before passage of the ADA.
- Discuss how activists worked for disabled rights and what legal protections they won.

Keep in mind that your essay should include an introduction, several paragraphs, and a conclusion. In the body of the essay, use evidence from at least three documents. Support your response with relevant facts, examples, and details. In developing your essay, be sure to keep these general definitions in mind:

- *Describe* means "to illustrate something in words or tell about it."
- *Discuss* means "to make observations about something using facts, reasoning, and argument; to present in some detail."

Source 1

Discrimination against the Deaf, from Enabling Acts: The Hidden Story of How the Americans with Disabilities Act Gave the Largest US Minority Its Rights, *Lennard J. Davis, 2015*

The son of hearing-impaired parents, Lennard J. Davis is a professor specializing in disability studies. On the 25th anniversary of the passage of the ADA, he wrote a book examining the impact of that historic law. Here, he describes the struggles faced by his parents and other disabled Americans.

My upbringing showed me firsthand how bad an impact discrimination against people with disabilities could be. As a child, I witnessed countless instances of hearing people treating my intelligent, talented, athletic Deaf parents as if they were lesser beings....

My parents were routinely excluded from places of public accommodation. We lived in a Bronx slum and when my parents applied to a more upscale housing development called Parkchester, their application was turned down. No Deaf people were allowed in. My father was a world-class athlete, but he was denied admittance to the New York Athletic Club for being Deaf (as well as Jewish). If either of my parents had wanted to drive a car, they would have needed an elaborate set of mirrors in the car. But even this accommodation wasn't possible, since insurance companies charged exorbitant rates for Deaf people (even though they had lower rates of accidents than the hearing).

In other words, although my parents were American citizens, they had few if any civil rights. Life was a series of insults, denigrations, and exclusions that they had to accept because there was no other choice. It was only within the Deaf community that they thrived and were fully appreciated.

The same was true not only for Deaf people, but also for people with any disabilities well into the twentieth century. Before civil rights legislation for people with disabilities, there was a huge catalog of abuses and barriers. As the largest minority, people with disabilities are among the poorest, least employed, and least educated of all minorities.

---

1. Describe two examples of discrimination faced by the author's parents.

2. What impact did being deaf have on the Davises' place in American society?

3. According to Davis, what disadvantages do people with all disabilities face? Why?

Source 2

Image of One 504 Sit-In, 1977

The disabled rights movement gained speed in the 1970s, often spearheaded by disabled Vietnam veterans. Activists were inspired by the earlier civil rights movement. In 1977, they staged a series of protests, demanding immediate enforcement of Section 504 of the Rehabilitation Act of 1973, which prohibited discrimination against the disabled in any program receiving federal funds.

1. What does this photograph show you about the protesters who took part in the 504 Sit-Ins?

On April 4, 1977, more than 50 protesters occupied the Denver offices of the Department of Health, Education, and Welfare. Similar sit-ins took place at federal buildings in many cities.

2. What effect do you think this protest had on federal offices? On lawmakers?

3. How does this photograph suggest that disabled rights advocates were inspired by the civil rights movement of the 1950s and 1960s?

Source 3

The "Capitol Crawl," Michael A. Winter

Passing the ADA was not easy. Many who opposed the law argued that it imposed costly requirements that would hurt businesses. As Congress debated, physically disabled activists staged a protest, abandoning their wheelchairs and crawling up the hundred steps leading to the Capitol. Here, Michael Winter describes the "Capitol Crawl."

. . . I thought about the many times that I had been discriminated against: being forced to go to a "special" segregated school instead of integrated ones, not being allowed on a [bus] because of my disability, and being told in a restaurant that "We don't serve disabled people." But I also had very positive thoughts about what a great life and great opportunities I had to that point. . . .

After the speeches, we started chanting "What do we want?" "ADA!" "When do we want it?" "NOW!" The chants became louder and louder, and ultimately my good friend Monica Hall told me that it was time to get out of my wheelchair and crawl up the steps to the [Capitol]. Monica took my wheelchair, smiled and said, "I'll meet you at the top!" I started to climb step by step towards the top.

At the very beginning, I looked up and thought that I would never make it. But right below me was a [seven-year-old] girl who was making the same climb. . . . I felt an obligation to be a role model for this girl and we ultimately made it to the top together.

Some people may have thought that it was undignified for people in wheelchairs to crawl in that manner, but I felt that it was necessary to show the country what kinds of things people with disabilities have to face on a day-to-day basis. We had to be willing to fight for what we believed in.

1. Why did protestors crawl up the steps of the Capitol?

2. What types of discrimination did Michael Winter face because he was in a wheelchair? What was your reaction when you read about his experiences?

3. Why do you think some people felt the protest was undignified? What was Winter's response? Explain who you agree with and why.

Source 4

President George H.W. Bush Signs the ADA, 1990

The Americans with Disabilities Act was passed by the Senate on July 13, 1990. Its chief Senate sponsor, Tom Harkin of Iowa, delivered his speech partly in sign language so his deaf brother could understand it. Two weeks later, President George H.W. Bush signed the bill into law in a White House ceremony attended by many disabled rights activists. The selection below is from Bush's remarks on the occasion.

Our success with this act proves that we are keeping faith with the spirit of our courageous forefathers who wrote in the Declaration of Independence: ``We hold these truths to be self-evident, that all men are created equal, that they are endowed by their Creator with certain unalienable rights." These words have been our guide for more than two centuries as we've labored to form our more perfect union. But tragically, for too many Americans, the blessings of liberty have been limited or even denied. The Civil Rights Act of '64 took a bold step towards righting that wrong. But the stark fact remained that people with disabilities were still victims of segregation and discrimination, and this was intolerable. Today's legislation brings us closer to that day when no Americans will ever again be deprived of their basic guarantee of life, liberty, and the pursuit of happiness.

This act is powerful in its simplicity. It will ensure that people with disabilities are given the basic guarantees for which they have worked so long and so hard: independence, freedom of choice, control of their lives, the opportunity to blend fully and equally into the rich mosaic of the American mainstream. Legally, it will provide our disabled community with a powerful expansion of protections and then basic civil rights. It will guarantee fair and just access to the fruits of American life which we all must be able to enjoy. And then, specifically, first the ADA ensures that employers covered by the act cannot discriminate against qualified individuals with disabilities. Second, the ADA ensures access to public accommodations such as restaurants, hotels, shopping centers, and offices. And third, the ADA ensures expanded access to transportation services. And fourth, the ADA ensures equivalent telephone services for people with speech or hearing impediments.

1. According to President Bush, how is the ADA a fulfillment of American values and ideals?

2. How does President Bush link the passage of the ADA to the earlier civil rights movement?

3. Choose two of the examples of discrimination described in Source 1 or Source 3. Explain how specific provisions of the ADA deal with each of these examples.

Lesson 1 The George W. Bush Presidency

CLOSE READING

Controversy in the 2000 Election

1. Summarize Why did the Democrats demand a recount in the 2000 presidential election?

The Bush Domestic and International Agenda

2. Summarize What were the goals behind the No Child Left Behind Act?

3. Analyze Causes Why did Bush withdraw the United States from the Kyoto Protocol? Do you agree with this decision?

The September 11 Terrorist Attacks

4. Analyze Style and Rhetoric How was Bush's speech after the 9/11 attacks similar to FDR's speech after Pearl Harbor?

5. **Analyze Sequence** Put the events of Bush's war on terror in chronological order and explain any connections between the events.

Bush's Second Term

6. **Identify Supporting Details** What was George W. Bush's most significant challenge in his second term? Support your answer with evidence from the text.

Digital Technology Impacts 21ˢᵗ Century Life

7. **Identify Effects** How did new technology affect work in offices in the 21ˢᵗ Century?

The Financial Crisis of 2008

8. **Identify Cause and Effect** Describe the chain of events that led to the financial crisis in September 2008.

Lesson 2 The Barack Obama Presidency

CLOSE READING

The 2008 Election

1. **Identify Cause and Effect** Explain at least one factor that contributed to Barack Obama's victory in the 2008 election.

President Obama Takes Action

2. **Analyze Issues** Describe the benefits and drawbacks of the Affordable Care Act.

3. **Draw Inferences** Why didn't the death of bin Laden end the threat of terrorism?

Obama's Second Term

4. **Determine Central Ideas** What was Barack Obama's most significant challenge during his second term?

A New Movement for Social Justice

5. Identify Causes What event helped to spark the #BlackLivesMatter movement? What deep-rooted problem in American history did the BLM movement protest?

6. Compare In what ways did both President Obama and Colin Kaepernick support the growing social justice movement?

The Environment

7. List Look at the chart "President Obama's Climate Action Plan". What were some of Obama's EPA regulatory goals?

Lesson 3 The Donald Trump Presidency

CLOSE READING

The 2016 Presidential Election

1. **Determine Central Ideas** Why would the idea of "draining the swamp" appeal to voters?

President Trump's National Agenda

2. **Compare** How did Trump's use of social media differ from previous presidents' approach?

3. **Describe** Describe President Obama's and President Trump's actions in relation to the Deferred Action for Childhood Arrivals (DACA) program. Use this chart to record your answers.

President Obama	President Trump

International Issues

4. Identify Effects What has Trump's "America First" policy meant for the U.S.'s relationship with China?

A Polarized Nation

5. Infer Why is Donald Trump considered to be a "polarizing" president?

6. Identify Effects How did the COVID-19 pandemic affect the daily lives of Americans in 2020?

The 2020 Election

7. Identify Effects How did the COVID-19 pandemic affect the 2020 election?

Lesson 4 Americans Look to the Future

CLOSE READING

The American Economy Today

1. Identify Effects How has the growth of the service sector changed the American economy?

Immigration Changes American Society

2. Infer Why have so many Latinos settled in Texas, New Mexico, Florida, and California?

American Demographics in Transition

3. Summarize How has the average American family changed in the last 50 years?

4. Analyze Interactions What factors have led to the underfunding of the United States' social welfare system?

Environmental Concerns Continue

5. Determine Central Idea What environmental issues does the West face?

Technology Transforms Life

6. Identify Effects How have advances in medical science and technology improved the health of Americans?

Concerns and Hope for the Future

7. Evaluate Of the issues discussed in this lesson, which causes you the most concern? What hopes for the future do you have related to that concern?

PRIMARY SOURCE EXPLORATION

The Impact of September 11, 2001

Introduction

For those who live through a significant moment in history, it is easy to remember just where you were and what the day was like when you heard the news. Those who were alive when the attack on Pearl Harbor during World War II, President Kennedy's and Martin Luther King's assassinations in the 1960s remember just where they were when they heard the news. For many Americans the day that lives vividly in their minds is September 11, 2001, or 9/11. On that day, terrorists attacked New York City's World Trade Center and the Pentagon building in Virginia, just outside of Washington, D.C. On the following pages you will read primary sources that give you a sense of the absolute shock that people felt on a that sunny September day as well as the repercussions that we still live with today.

Document-Based Writing Activity

Analyze the following four sources and then use information from the documents and your knowledge of U.S. history to write an essay in which you

- Discuss the events of 9/11 and how it changed the United States.
- Evaluate steps the United States took to secure the nation after 9/11.

Keep in mind that your essay should include an introduction, several paragraphs, and a conclusion. In the body of the essay, use evidence from at least three documents. Support your response with relevant facts, examples, and details. In developing your essay, be sure to keep these general definitions in mind:

- *Discuss* means "to observations about something using facts, reasoning, and argument; to present in some details."
- *Evaluate* means "to examine and judge the significance, worth, or condition of; to determine the value of."

Source 1

Statement by President George W. Bush in his Address to the Nation, September 11, 2001, 8:30

After the attack on the World Trade Center and the Pentagon, President George W. Bush addressed the nation in a televised speech in the evening. This is an excerpt from that speech.

Today, our fellow citizens, our way of life, our very freedom came under attack in a series of deliberate and deadly terrorist acts. The victims were in airplanes, or in their offices; secretaries, businessmen and women, military and federal workers; moms and dads, friends and neighbors. Thousands of lives were suddenly ended by evil, despicable acts of terror.

The pictures of airplanes flying into buildings, fires burning, huge structures collapsing, have filled us with disbelief, terrible sadness, and a quiet, unyielding anger. These acts of mass murder were intended to frighten our nation into chaos and retreat. But they have failed; our country is strong.

A great people has been moved to defend a great nation. Terrorist attacks can shake the foundations of our biggest buildings, but they cannot touch the foundation of America. These acts shattered steel, but they cannot dent the steel of American resolve.

America was targeted for attack because we're the brightest beacon for freedom and opportunity in the world. And no one will keep that light from shining.

Today, our nation saw evil, the very worst of human nature. And we responded with the best of America—with the daring of our rescue workers, with the caring for strangers and neighbors who came to give blood and help in any way they could. . . .

The search is underway for those who are behind these evil acts. I've directed the full resources of our intelligence and law enforcement communities to find those responsible and to bring them to justice. We will make no distinction between the terrorists who committed these acts and those who harbor them. . . .

This is a day when all Americans from every walk of life unite in our resolve for justice and peace. America has stood down enemies before, and we will do so this time. None of us will ever forget this day. Yet, we go forward to defend freedom and all that is good and just in our world.

Thank you. Good night, and God bless America.

---

1. How does President Bush describe the objectives of the terrorists?

2. Why was Bush confident that Americans would rise above the events of 9/11?

3. Explain what Bush meant when he said "America was targeted for attack because we're the brightest beacon for freedom and opportunity in the world. And no one will keep that light from shining."

Source 2

Ten Years Later: An Interview with a Firefighter About 9/11, September 2011

The following interview was conducted ten years after September 2001. The excerpt from this interview illustrates that ten years after the event, details of that day and the days that followed are etched in the minds of those who lived through it.

Dennis: I'm speaking to Charles about the events of September 11, 2001. You were a firefighter at the time, correct? What were you doing when you first heard about the attack?

Charles: Correct. . . . I had just left my job at the emergency operations center at the FDNY (Fire Department of New York) after a 24-hour tour.

Dennis: [Were] you or anyone you know personally involved in the events that day?

Charles: I responded back to the emergency operations center. I worked another 48 hours there before being relieved. From my personal account I knew 75 of the firefighters that were killed that day. . . .

At the emergency operations center we were the nucleus of the operations for the entire fire department while it tried to get back on its feet, having lost so many people. There was still a city that had to be protected from the regular day-to-day activities that the fire department handles. ... We basically worked 24- or 48-hour shifts straight. ... and we immediately began to arrange for funeral and memorial services. [The] night of 9/11, I spent six hours answering the phone of people calling in and wondering if there was any word about their loved ones. That was a very tortuous six hours. There were people crying. There were retired firefighters begging for information on their sons. It was a very emotional day.

Dennis: How do you think the attacks on September 11 have changed America and hope?

Charles: Well, we've rearranged our focus, having probably been a little smug prior to this thinking we could not be attacked on our own shores. I believe this certainly changed the minds of at least the people in public service. Perhaps many Americans now that it's ten years after the fact, have gone back to business as usual. And sometimes I think in people's minds—oh yeah, yeah, that was that terrible thing that happened some time ago. But those of us in public service, for the most part, [are] ever aware and constantly learning.

---

1. How does Charles describe the emergency operations center? How did the center respond to 9/11?

2. What do you think was the most difficult part of Charles's job on 9/11?

3. How does Charles think that 9/11 changed America and Americans?

Source 3

Debate in the Senate on the USA PATRIOT Act of 2001, October 25, 2001

About six weeks after 9/11 the USA Patriot Act was passed by Congress and signed into law by President Bush in October 2001. In the House and the Senate, the bill passed easily. In the Senate, there was a single "no" vote from Russ Feingold a Democrat from Wisconsin. His views and those of Orrin Hatch, a Republican from Utah, appear below.

SEN. RUSS FEINGOLD (D-WI):... As we address this bill, ... we are especially mindful of the terrible events of September 11 and beyond, which led to this bill's proposal and its quick consideration in the Congress. . . .

I have concluded that this bill still does not strike the right balance between empowering law enforcement and protecting civil liberties. ...
[Law] enforcement agencies can search homes and offices without notifying the owner prior to the search. The longstanding practice under the fourth amendment of serving a warrant prior to executing a search could be easily avoided . . . because the government would simply have to show that it had "reasonable cause to believe" that providing notice 'may' seriously jeopardize an investigation." This is a significant infringement on personal liberty. . . . If you're not home, and the police have received permission to do a "sneak and peek" search, they can come in your house, look around, and leave, and may never have to tell you that ever happened. ...

SEN. ORRIN HATCH (R-UT): I rise to address briefly a couple of the points made by the distinguished Senator from Wisconsin. First, what he called a "sneak and peek" search warrant, these warrants are already used throughout the United States, throughout our whole country. . . . Let me be clear. Courts already allow warrants under our fourth amendment. It is totally constitutional. . . .
Second, to respond to the suggestion that the legislation is not properly mindful of our constitutional liberties—my friend from Wisconsin talks theoretically about maybe the loss of some civil liberties—I would like to talk concretely about the loss of liberty of almost 6,000 people because of the terrorist acts on September 11. I am a little bit more concerned right now about their loss of life.
Thousands of Americans died that day [September 11], thousands. That is real. We have been told there may be some other actions taken by terrorists. That may be real. To the extent that may be real, we sure want to make sure our law enforcement people, within the constraints of the Constitution, have the optimum [best] law enforcement tools they need to do the job. [...]

1. To which amendment did senators Feingold and Hatch refer? What is the content of this bill?

2. What are each of the senators' points of view about what they refer to as "sneak and peek" warrants?

3. Based on the senators' points of view about the bill, what may be some pros and cons about the USA PATRIOT ACT?

Source Exploration ▪ America in the Twenty-First Century

Source 4

Image of TSA agents in an airport, 2010

The image below shows Transportation Security Administration (TSA) agents. The TSA was created as a result of the 9/11 attacks and has remained to safeguard passengers in the airports. Most travelers are familiar with agents like the ones shown in the image, but there are TSA agents working behind the scenes to check passenger lists for people who may be on a security threat list, to check suspicious behavior, and to make other assessments. A division of TSA sends security officers to patrol railways, mass transit systems, and shipping areas.

TSA agents stand ready to screen airplane passengers' hand luggage and scan their bodies to check for explosives, weapons, or other prohibited items.

1. Why was the Transportation Security Administration created?

2. What equipment do you recognize from this image?

3. Do you think that TSA agents are still necessary in airports and in other places? Why or why not?

Photography

Topic 1

10: Photo12/Archives Snark/Alamy Stock Photo

Topic 3

39: Alpha Stock/Alamy Stock Photo

Topic 5

70: Everett Historical/Shutterstock

Topic 6

89: N. Currier/Library of Congress Prints and Photographs Division Washington, D.C.[LC-USZC2-3760]

Topic 7

107: Currier & Ives/Library of Congress Prints and Photographs Division Washington[LC-USZC2-2571]

Topic 9

135L: The New York Public Library/Art Resource, NY; **135R:** The New York Public Library/Art Resource, NY

Topic 10

146: Sueddeutsche Zeitung Photo/Alamy Stock Photo

Topic 11

168L: History and Art Collection/Alamy Stock Photo; **168R:** F. Victor Gillam/Circa Images/Glasshouse Images/Alamy Stock Photo

Topic 12

189: Courtesy Yale Library Beinecke Collection

Topic 13

203: George P. Clements papers (Collection 118), Library Special Collections, Charles E. Young Research Library, UCLA.; **205:** John Parrot/Stocktrek Images/Alamy Stock Photo

Topic 14

227: Corbis

Topic 16

261: AP Images

Topic 17

273: Julian C. Wilson/AP Images

Topic 18

288: Ralph Crane/The Life Picture Collection/Getty Images; **291:** Bettmann/UPI/Getty Images

Topic 19

304: John Prieto/The Denver Post/Getty Images

Topic 20

319: Scott Olson/Staff/Getty Images

Text Acknowledgements

Topic 1

Excerpt from: The voyages of Giovanni da Verrazzano, 1524–1528 (1970), "Giovanni da Verrazzano, Letter to King Francis I of France 8 July 1524 Verrazano." by Wroth, Lawrence C. (Lawrence Counselman), 1884-1970. Published by Yale University Press. Reprinted with permission.; Quote from: First Encounters of the Ho-Chunk Nation and the French. Account recorded by Paul Radin, published in Thirty-Seventh Annual Report of the Bureau of American Ethnology, 1915–1916 (Washington, DC: Government Printing Office, 1923), pp. 67–69.; Excerpt from: (MICMAC)Algonguin Indians Encounter with Europeans, 1680. New Relation of Gaspesia by Father Chrestien Le Glercq, translated by William F. Ganong. Published by The Champlain Society, 1910.

Topic 2

Excerpt from: The Bloudy Tenent of Persecution for the Cause of Conscience by Roger Williams (1644; reprinted London, 1848); Excerpt from: Theodore de la Guard [Nathaniel Ward], The Simple Cobbler of Aggawamm in America (London, 1647), reprinted in Hart, ed., American History Told by Contemporaries, vol. 1 (New York, 1898); Excerpt from: "A Letter Concerning Toleration" by John Locke, 1689.

Topic 3

03: Excerpt from: The Adventures of A Revolutionary Soldier by Joseph Plumb Martin, 1830.; Quote from: Regulations for the Order and Discipline of the Troops of the United States, Friedrich Wilhelm von Steuben.; Excerpt from The Adventures of A Revolutionary Soldier by Joseph Plumb Martin, 1830.

Topic 4

Excerpt from: Notes on the Debates in the Federal Convention, James Madison, August 22, 1787.; Excerpt from: Speech by James Iredell at the Convention of North Carolina, July 1788.; Quote from:–Letter from William Rotch, Sr., to Moses Brown, November 1787"; Quote from: Speech by Charles Pinckney, January 1788". Max Farrand,

The Records of the Federal Convention of 1787, vol. 3. Published by Yale University Press, 1911.; Data from chart: John McCusker and Russell Menard (1985), pp. 108, 130, 172, 199. The Economy of British America, 1607–1789. Chapel Hill, NC: University of North Carolina Press.

Topic 5

05: Excerpt from: "Pacificus III" and "Pacificus VII," Alexander Hamilton, 1793.; Statement by the Student Nonviolent Coordinating Committee on the War in Vietnam from a Letter by Harry Belafonte, January 6, 1966.; Excerpt from Address by Ambassador Susan Rice at the United States Institute of Peace, January 10, 2017.

Topic 6

Excerpt from "Matamoros Proclamation," General Francisco Mejia, March 18, 1846 Messages of the President of the United States: with the Correspondence, Therewith Communicated, between the Secretary of War and Other Officers of the Government, on the Subject of the Mexican War (Washington, D.C.: Wendell and Van Benthuysen 1848), 127–129.; Excerpt from: Speech in the United States House of Representatives, Abraham Lincoln, January 12, 1848.; Public Domain

Topic 7

Excerpt from: Mississippi Declaration of Secession written by Lucius Quintas Cincinnatus Lamar (II) US Congress, January 1861.; Excerpt from: Memoirs of Mrs. Clay, of Alabama, Covering Social and Political Life in Washington and the South, 1853-66, Published by Doubleday, Page & Company, 1904; Excerpt from: The Union and How to Save It, Frederick Douglass, February 1861.

Topic 8

Reconstruction Reassessed by E.L. Godkin. The Nation. **13:** 336 (December 7, 1871); "Testing the 15th Amendment: Milton Claiborne Nicholas and the Legacy of the First Black Voters" U.S. Congress, February 25, 1869.; Excerpt from: Smith v. Allwright, U.S. Supreme Court, 1944.; Excerpt From Shelby County v. Holder and the memory of civil rights progress by Abigail Perkiss, 2013.

Topic 9

Interview with Mrs. John Donnelly on Pioneer Life in Nebraska, November 1938. Library of Congress Manuscript Division, WPA Federal Writers' Project Collection.; "A Chinese Immigrant Tells of Labor in a New Land." by Lee Chew; Guide for the Immigrant Italian in the United States of America, 1911. Doubleday, Page & Co.

Topic 10

Excerpt from: "Buffalo Hunting," Harper's Weekly, December 14, 1867.; Excerpt from: Speech: "Bright Eyes" by Susette La Flesche, 1881.; Excerpt from: State of the Union Address. President Benjamin Harrison on Indian Policy, December 3, 1889.; Reprinted from Black Elk Speaks: Complete Edition by John G. Neihardt by permission of the University of Nebraska Press. Copyright 2014 by the Board of Regents of the University of Nebraska

Topic 11

Excerpt from Benevolent Assimilation Proclamation, William McKinley, 1898. Published by The Knickerbocker Press, 1913.; Excerpt from: Manifesto Against Imperialism, Emilio Aguinaldo, 1899. Published by the U.S. Government Printing Office, 1899.; Excerpt from: Mark Twain, The Greatest American Humorist, Returning Home, New York World, London, 10/6/1900.

Topic 12

Excerpt from: "Harlem, Mecca of the New Negro" by Alain Locke from Survey Graphic, March 1925.; "Spring to See Greatest Migration in History" Copyright © The Chicago Defender, February 21, 1925.; Letter from Rampy J. Burdick to Attorney General John G. Sargeant, 1928.

Topic 13

Quote from The Mexican Farm Labor Program, 1942–1964: Government-Administered Labor Market Insurance for Farmers by Wayne A. Grove. Agricultural History Vol. 70, No. 2, Twentieth-Century Farm Policies (Spring, 1996), pp. 302–320.; Interview with Agustín Martínez Olivares. Reprinted with permission from Dr. Yolanda Leyva. Institute of Oral History.; Letter from Pablo Guerrero to the Los Angeles County Clerk, May 28, 1934. From Decade of Betrayal: Mexican Repatriation in the 1930s by Francisco E. Balderrama and Raymond Rodriguez. Copyright © 1995. University of New Mexico Press, 1995.